SMALL GEORGIAN HOUSES
AND THEIR DETAILS

BROWN HOUSE, REIGATE: PORCH.

SMALL GEORGIAN HOUSES AND THEIR DETAILS

1750-1820

IN TWO PARTS
I. EXTERIORS   II. INTERIORS AND DETAILS

By
Stanley C. Ramsey, F.R.I.B.A.
and
J. D. M. Harvey

With a foreword by J. M. Richards

The Architectural Press: London

*First published in two separate volumes
under the title of* Small Houses of
the Late Georgian Period, *1750-1820.
Volume I (exteriors) published 1919,
reprinted 1919 and 1924. Volume II
(details and interiors) published 1923.
This edition (with both volumes under
one cover and under a new title) published
1972.*

SBN 0 85139 250 4
© *The Architectural Press, London,* 1972

Printed in Great Britain by Balding and Mansell Ltd., Wisbech, Cambs.

FOREWORD to the new edition

THIS splendid collection of photographs and drawings, out of print for many years, is well worth reissuing. There is increasing interest in, and demand for, houses of the type Stanley Ramsey sought out more than 50 years ago. He said, in his introduction to the first volume, that they were rapidly disappearing. That process has continued ever since, and several of the examples he was able to photograph exist no longer.

In recent years, however, the faster rate of destruction brought about by the rebuilding of towns and cities, by towns expanding into previously rural areas and by such activities as road-widening even in areas that have remained rural, has been to a great extent balanced by the legislation, introduced since Ramsey's day, under which old buildings are listed and to some extent protected, and by our greater interest in environmental values. This has led, for example, to the Civic Amenities Act of 1967, which encourages the conservation of groups of modest, individually unimportant buildings such as give a consistent character and historical continuity to many of our towns but were at the mercy of the developers when only the major monuments were protected by law.

It is to be hoped that the reissue of this book may prove useful when late Georgian buildings are being restored or adapted to new uses. When it was first published, Ramsey's book was no doubt much used as a source of ideas and a copybook of details by architects designing new houses, or by clients anxious to show their architects the style of house they wanted; for houses were then invariably modelled on the style of some previous era and the Georgian was enjoying a particularly successful revival. The Georgian-style house, with its straightforward plan, its commodious rooms and its basic simplicity of form, was adaptable to contemporary needs and was easy to furnish and equip with modern heating, lighting and plumbing. Stanley Ramsey himself, with his partner Adshead, was one of the most skilful of the Georgian revival domestic architects.

Foreword

But now we think differently about building in the styles of past periods. Speculative builders' "bijou" houses with pretentious Georgian doorways and bay windows still sometimes rear their specious heads, and it would be regrettable if the reissue of this book gave encouragement to such ineptitudes. The book's role should now be to arouse interest in the quality and variety of the small houses still to be found all over the country, and assist the process of preserving and restoring them. If we no longer believe in constructing imitations of Georgian houses, we value even more highly those that survive. We even see, in the rationality of their design and in their use of standardized elements, a forerunner of some modern ideas; their simplicity, reticence and elegance are in tune with the modern aesthetic. The number of architects who choose to live in houses of the kind illustrated here is proof of the response they unfailingly evoke.

The fact that Ramsey regarded these houses as exemplars of style rather than as an historical record no doubt explains why he treated his material purely pictorially. He gives no plans or information about accommodation or construction, and he has made only a few attempts to discover the names of the architects responsible. In many cases there probably were none, the houses being run up by a builder with the help of pattern-books and traditional local practices. It is therefore surprising to find Ramsey stating in his introduction that "it would seem to have been the rule rather than the exception for an intending builder to engage the services of an architect . . . the professional architect was a matter of course called in for advice and assistance". That may have been so for mansions of some pretension, but not for the ordinary small house or cottage to which Ramsey devotes many of his pictures.

Nor does Ramsey give the dates of the houses he illustrates. There is simply the implication, in the title of the book, that all the examples are later than 1750 and earlier than 1820; and his description of late Georgian as a period still to be properly appreciated is interesting, since we are not nowadays aware of much difference in this respect between early and late Georgian. Late Georgian houses he says, "are still so numerous and cover so large an area that it is not to be wondered at if we accept them as entirely commonplace, and feel that, as such, they require no effort of comprehension or appreciation—that they are in fact outside the range of our artistic interests". Today, even though our record of caring for our Georgian inheritance is hardly one to be proud of, late Georgian is valued as much as early and cared for as well—or as badly.

Incidentally, Ramsey's choice of limiting dates is something of a puzzle. 1750—mid-century—is fair enough as an arbitrary line between early Georgian and late; but why stop at 1820? If he wanted to treat Regency as a separate style, then 1820 is too late—the Regency began in 1810. If he did

Foreword

not want to do so—which seems likely, since several of the houses he includes could be described as Regency, and in his introduction to the second volume he comments that "the glories of the eighteenth-century house craftsmanship gave place to the trivialities of the Victorian . . ."—then 1820 is too early; George IV died only in 1830. In any case several of his examples could well be later than 1820.

Looking at Ramsey's book one remarks, in fact, a number of differences in outlook between the time of publication (the book was issued in two volumes, in 1919 and 1923) and today. One such difference is indicated by the word "small" in his title. Evidently what we would call a largish house was still small by the spacious standards of fifty years ago. Ramsey includes many houses that only a rich man could afford to live in now, and that only a very large family would require—for example Thorncroft Manor, Leatherhead (Plate 32), Ashley House, Epsom (Plate 1), Garrick Villa, Hampton-on-Thames (Plate 16) and Northfield House, Henley (plate 13), with its 15 windows in a row on each storey of its main façade. These are hardly our idea of a small house.

Another difference is our more tolerant attitude to sophisticated deviations from what Ramsey regarded as the true Georgian style, although—as he himself admits—minor changes, chiefly the result of the personal influence of leading architects like Adam and Soane, were taking place all the time. Ramsey is particularly hard on the Greek Revival, which is surprising in view of the value he attaches to precision and elegance. He illustrates several houses dating from the early part of the nineteenth century which have Greek detail, but describes them as bearing witness to the "efforts of the well-meaning but heavy-handed archaeologist" and adds that "the immediate effect of all this learning on the domestic architecture of this country was disastrous". It is characteristic of the interests of his day that Ramsey clearly chose his examples to a great extent for the quality and variety of their detail, and this gives additional value as a record to his collection of photographs.

Something should be said about the original edition of the book. The title of the first volume was *Small Houses of the Late Georgian Period: 1750–1820*. The author was given as Stanley C. Ramsey and publication was by Technical Journals Ltd (the predecessors of the Architectural Press). The date on the title-page was 1919. There was a 16-page introduction, reprinted here, followed by 100 plates bearing 130 photographs—all of exteriors, or exterior details such as doorways. Only a few photographers' names were given.

The second volume was published in 1923, with the sub-title, *Details and Interiors*, and with J. D. M. Harvey's name added to Ramsey's. Harvey was responsible for the elegant measured drawings—mostly of

Foreword

interior details but including some external elevations—which occupied 40 pages. The title-page (on which "Architectural Press" already replaced "Technical Journals") also stated that the volume contained "Fifty Photographs by F. R. Yerbury". There were in fact 77 photographs, and there is no indication of which were by Yerbury. This new (1972) edition combines both volumes in one, and prints the illustrations, originally printed on one side of the paper only, on both sides.

Finally, something should be said about the authors. Stanley C. Ramsey was born in 1882 and died in 1968. For thirty years of his professional life, from 1911 onwards, he practised in partnership with Professor S. D. Adshead (1868–1946), the distinguished town-planner. They were architects to the Duchy of Cornwall Estate, and together they designed an ambitious reconstruction of the Duchy's housing estate at Kennington in a discreet but scholarly neo-Georgian idiom. Ramsey also wrote a book on Inigo Jones. He was vice-president of the RIBA in 1944–45. J. D. M. Harvey, who was born in Canada in 1895, was well known as a draughtsman and since 1924 his water-colour renderings have been much in demand by architects and have been seen year after year on the walls of the Architecture Room at the Royal Academy.

London, 1972   J. M. Richards

I. EXTERIORS

LIST OF PLATES

Frontispiece. BROWN HOUSE, REIGATE: PORCH.
Plate 1. ASHLEY HOUSE, EPSOM.
„ 2. ASHLEY HOUSE, EPSOM: PORCH.
„ 3. HOUSE ON HOLYWELL HILL, ST. ALBANS.
„ 4. BROWN HOUSE, REIGATE: GARDEN FRONT.
„ 5. SURREY LODGE, DENMARK HILL, LONDON, S.E.
„ 6. HOUSES IN OWEN STREET, HEREFORD.
SHOP IN OWEN STREET, HEREFORD.
„ 7. DOORWAY TO CHANDOS HOUSE, HEREFORD.
DOORWAY IN OWEN STREET, HEREFORD.
„ 8. WANTLEY MANOR, HENFIELD, SUSSEX.
„ 9. HOUSE AT HENFIELD, SUSSEX.
„ 10. HOUSES IN DOYLE ROAD, ST. PETER PORT, GUERNSEY.
„ 11. HOUSE IN DOYLE ROAD, ST. PETER PORT, GUERNSEY: GARDEN FRONT.
„ 12. HOUSE ON THE SAUMAREZ ROAD, GUERNSEY.
„ 13. NORTHFIELD HOUSE, HENLEY.
„ 14. "THE WICK," RICHMOND HILL, SURREY.
„ 15. "HOLLYDALE," KESTON, KENT.
„ 16. GARRICK VILLA, HAMPTON-ON-THAMES.
„ 17. HOUSES ON KENNINGTON GREEN, LONDON, S.E.
„ 18. DOORWAY, KENNINGTON GREEN, LONDON, S.E.
„ 19. DOORWAY AND BALCONY, STAFFORD HOUSE, UPPER KENNINGTON LANE, S.E.
„ 20. STONE HOUSE, LEWISHAM.
THE GRANGE, ST. PETER'S STREET, ST. ALBANS.
„ 21. PORCH, STONE HOUSE, LEWISHAM, LONDON, S.E.
„ 22. HOUSE ON THE PARADE, WEYMOUTH.
„ 23. HOUSES IN CASTLE STREET, HEREFORD.
TERRACE OF HOUSES IN WIDMARSH STREET, HEREFORD.
„ 24. HOUSE IN WELL WALK, HAMPSTEAD, LONDON, N.W.
„ 25. KENT HOUSE, THE MALL, HAMMERSMITH.
„ 26. STRAWBERRY HOUSE, THE MALL, CHISWICK.
„ 27. TWO LONDON DOORWAYS: KENNINGTON ROAD, S.E.
THE MALL, CHISWICK, W.
„ 28. THE VICARAGE, 22 LOWER MALL, HAMMERSMITH.
„ 29. BRAMPTON HOUSE, CHURCH STREET, CHISWICK.
„ 30. LINDEN HOUSE, THE MALL, HAMMERSMITH, LONDON.
„ 31. ASGILL HOUSE, RICHMOND, SURREY.
„ 32. THORNCROFT MANOR, LEATHERHEAD, SURREY.
„ 33. TOLL HOUSE, HENLEY.
„ 34. DOORWAY, ANCASTER HOUSE, RICHMOND HILL, SURREY.
PORTICO IN RUSKIN PARK, DENMARK HILL.
„ 35. DOORWAY, QUARRY STREET, GUILDFORD.
DOORWAY, THE GREEN, RICHMOND, SURREY.
„ 36. WOODBINE COTTAGE, PETERSHAM, SURREY.
„ 37. HOUSES IN CHISWICK LANE, LONDON, W.
„ 38. PAIR OF HOUSES, QUARRY STREET, GUILDFORD.
„ 39. PAIR OF HOUSES AT COBHAM, SURREY.
„ 40. FARM-HOUSE AT COBHAM, SURREY.
„ 41. DOORWAY IN HIGH STREET, MARLOW.
DOORWAY IN ST. PETER'S STREET, ST. ALBANS.
„ 42. HOUSE AT COBHAM, SURREY.
„ 43. "THE RUNNING HORSES" INN, MICKLEHAM, SURREY.
„ 44. HOUSES IN BROAD STREET, STAMFORD.
„ 45. THE WHITE LION HOTEL, COBHAM, SURREY.
„ 46. WEATHERBOARDED HOUSES AT ASHTEAD, SURREY.
„ 47. WEATHERBOARDED COTTAGES AT CAPEL, SURREY.
„ 48. WEATHERBOARDED COTTAGES AT ST. ALBANS.
IN BARROW ROAD, STREATHAM.
„ 49. ELM HOUSE, HENLEY.
HOUSE AT HAMPSTEAD.

List of Plates

Plate 50. Two Houses in High Street, Marlow.
,, 51. Houses Facing Alfred Square, Deal.
,, 52. Cottages in Fishpool Street, St. Albans.
Cottages in Sandridge Road, St. Albans.
,, 53. River House to Syon House, Isleworth.
,, 54. Entrance to House in Camberwell Road, London, S.E.
Verandah on Houses, St. Albans.
,, 55. Porch, Blackheath Hill, London, S.E.
,, 56. Doorway, Lower Kennington Lane, London S.E.
,, 57. House at Esher, Surrey.
,, 58. No. 6 Southwood Lane, Highgate, London, N.
,, 59. Two Houses on Ham Common, Surrey.
,, 60. Langham House, Ham, Surrey.
House in St. Peter's Street, St. Albans.
,, 61. Porch to Southwood House, Highgate, London.
,, 62. House on The Terrace, Barnes.
,, 63. House on The Terrace, Barnes.
,, 64. Porch, "The Limes," Kingston-on-Thames.
,, 65. Milbourne House, Barnes.
,, 66. Cottages in Southwood Lane, Hampstead.
Porch to House in Church Row, Hampstead.
,, 67. House at Thaxted, Essex.
Cottages at Stokesley, Yorkshire.
,, 68. Council House, Barnes.
,, 69. Terrace on Richmond Hill.
,, 70. Trellis Porch at Dorking.
Trellis Porch at Leatherhead.
,, 71. The Paragon, Blackheath, London, S.E.
,, 72. The Paragon, Blackheath, London, S.E.: Detail of Wing.
,, 73. Two Houses at Blackheath.
,, 74. Cottages, Pond Lane, Lower Clapton.
Cottages at Merton, Surrey.
,, 75. House at Truro.
,, 76. House on Champion Hill, London, S.E.
,, 77. Durlstone Manor, Champion Hill.
,, 78. House in Bell Street, Henley.
,, 79. The Elms, Epsom.
,, 80. House at Horsham, Surrey.
,, 81. House at Kennington Oval.
,, 82. Shop at Dorking, Surrey.
,, 83. Shop in Widmarsh Street, Hereford.
Shop near Cathedral, Hereford.
,, 84. House in High Street, Marlow.
House at Star Cross, Devonshire.
,, 85. Two Houses in Kennington Road, London, S.E.
,, 86. Doctor's House, New Cross, London, S.E.
,, 87. Cedar Lodge, Blackheath, London, S.E.
Office, Bury Street, Bloomsbury, London, W.
,, 88. Terrace on Richmond Hill.
Terrace in Sheen Lane, Mortlake.
,, 89. Hurst Cottage, Hampton, Middlesex.
,, 90. House at St. Margaret's, Middlesex.
House at St. Albans.
,, 91. House at Herne Hill.
Pair of Houses in Water Lane, Brixton.
,, 92. Cottages at Giggshill Green, near Esher, Surrey.
,, 93. House on the Hagley Road, Birmingham.
,, 94. Halnaker Lodge, Coldharbour Lane, Brixton, London, S.W.
,, 95. "Oakfield," Dulwich Village.
,, 96. Morden Lodge, Morden, Surrey.
,, 97. Berkeley House, Corporation Street, Rochester.
,, 98. Shops in Woburn Place, London, W.C.
,, 99. Drayton House, St. Margaret's, Middlesex.
,, 100. Doorway to House at Hampton, Middlesex.
Three Doorways in High Street, Rochford, Essex.

SHOP FRONT AT BATH.
From a Pencil Sketch by Harold Falkner.

INTRODUCTION

SO much has been written about and around our domestic architecture that it would appear on first thoughts to be almost impossible to add anything that could be of general interest. There is, however, one period whose buildings have not perhaps received so ample a recognition as they merit; more particularly the houses that were built in the latter half of the eighteenth century and the early years of the nineteenth, which for the sake of a convenient nomenclature may be called the Late Georgian period.

Modern writers have in general been singularly reticent both with regard to the work and the authors of it, except in so far as the larger and more important buildings are concerned; and the smaller houses, as compared with the great town and country mansions, have for the most part been ignored. There are many reasons which account for this seeming indifference both in the professional and lay mind. Our renewed interest in the house and home dates from the later days of the Gothic revival; and, as a natural sequence, our attention was for a long time devoted almost exclusively to the earlier styles which were related to or in sympathy with it. This later work was in point of time too near the years of the revivalists for them to have felt much interest in it, and for the most part they regarded it with a scarcely concealed dislike; whilst we moderns, although we do not view it with the repugnance of our fathers, feel perhaps that it is not quite sufficiently hallowed by the sanctity of age or of a geographical remoteness such as might give it the glamour of the strange and foreign.

Again, the buildings erected between the years of, say, 1750 and 1820 which remain to us, though, alas! rapidly disappearing

Introduction

in certain districts, are still so numerous and cover so large an area that it is not to be wondered at if we accept them as entirely commonplace, and feel that, as such, they require no effort of comprehension or appreciation—that they are in fact outside the range of our artistic interests. We know them only as we have known some familiar yet alien object in a street through which we have constantly passed: familiar in that we have seen it many times, but unconsciously; alien inasmuch as we do not really know it. This is an experience common to most of us. We may walk along a certain road nearly every morning of the year, and feel that we are familiar with every detail of every building in it; yet on some particular day something will attract our attention—a knocker, a fanlight, or even a whole façade, which, although we had passed it on many previous occasions, we had never properly observed till then. So it is with these houses; we meet them at every turn, they crowd amongst our most familiar associations. Perhaps it has been this very familiarity which has bred the indifference; but there they are — quiet, retiring, unobtrusive, and essentially delightful.

They are for the most part formal in type, though not always in the disposition and treatment of their parts; whilst there is scarcely a building so entirely formal that it does not in a lesser or greater degree owe something to that which is incidental. On the other hand, where large areas have been built upon at one and the same time, and the treatment of each building is separate and unrelated, the total effect of the street or district must owe much of its success or failure to causes which are in the main accidental. It is between these extremes in principle—of formality, which carried to excess produces wearisome repetition, and informality, the over-indulgence of which means confusion and anarchy—that some of the happiest results have been obtained. In the study of the buildings which form the subject of this volume, there is to be observed a happy blend of both the formal and the informal, though this informality cannot in the majority of instances be said to be altogether the result of accident, but is rather due, if the phrase be permissible, to a considered carelessness.

Thus we find the most severe and uncompromising of elevations set off with a slight trellis porch or verandah, treated with the greatest possible freedom; or a weather-boarded cottage having windows and entrance door carried out with the most perfect precision.

For the most part these houses were designed by men of taste and capability; it would seem to have been the rule rather than

Introduction

the exception for an intending builder to engage the services of an architect to design and superintend the building of his home. Speculative building was in its extreme infancy; and, following the aristocratic example of the time, the professional architect was as a matter of course called in for advice and assistance. That great body of well-to-do lower middle class which has of recent years been so extensively provided for by what is known as "private enterprise," did not at this time exist; the man of the working class had his house provided for him by the great town or country landlord, and the employment of the architect for all building affairs was practically universal. As a natural result, these houses, viewed collectively, show a far higher standard of design than has since prevailed; and although they are remarkable for a wide diversity of treatment, there is a strong family likeness between them.

Again, the publication of books of designs for all classes of buildings by the architects of the late eighteenth century provided useful models for the small country builders, who undoubtedly made great use of them. In the introduction to his book of designs, published in 1767, John Crunden employs the following description:—

"Convenient and ornamental architecture, consisting of original designs for plans, elevations, and sections; beginning with the farm-house and regularly ascending to the most grand and magnificent villa, calculated both for town and country, and to suit all persons in any station of life."

The last phrase in this ingenious preamble throws an interesting sidelight on the jealously observed distinctions in the society of that time. Nearly all our large towns and cities which date from pre-industrial days contain numerous examples of late eighteenth-century buildings, and many of our country towns and villages almost entirely owe their charm—that appearance of restful quietness—to the long horizontal lines of this later work. London has many built-up areas exclusively belonging to this time, from the great town houses of the West-end streets and squares to the lesser-known examples to be found in the immediate as well as in the more remote suburbs. Particularly is this the case with that part of the capital which lies to the south of the Thames. This district has in a large measure escaped the modernization of recent years, which has painfully transformed many of the residential suburbs in the northern sections into wildernesses of red brick and terra-cotta. Those suburbs more immediate to the centre of London contain streets and squares the houses of which, allowing

Introduction

for the difference in size, correspond with the larger and better-known town house proper. There is to be found the continuous terrace with groups of formal dwellings, the separate units of which together form a complete scheme of design. Many such streets and squares are to be found in the little-known districts of Lambeth, Kennington, Pentonville, and Hackney, with here and there an isolated house or pair of houses proclaiming their superior-social claims in a design distinct in itself, but related in character and style to the surrounding buildings. It is with these more individual houses that this book is particularly concerned: the single house, often standing in its own grounds, with a quality of its own; and these form the majority of the examples illustrated in the accompanying plates. Houses of this kind are to be found in outlying districts of London such as Brixton, Dulwich, Greenwich, Blackheath, Barnes, Mortlake, Richmond, Ham, and Kingston on the south; and at Hampstead, Highgate, Hammersmith, and Chiswick on the north side of the Thames, as well as in the country towns and villages, with here and there an isolated straggler or small group bordering on some old coaching road.

The last quarter of the eighteenth century witnessed a revival of interest in the country and country-side pursuits. The writings of Jean Jacques Rousseau, that sophisticated missioner of the simple life, which could best be realized away from the towns, had seized hold of the French imagination, and afterwards gradually penetrated the slower intelligence of our own countrymen. One immediate effect of this was to cause a migratory movement amongst the wealthier citizens towards what was then the open country; and a desire for a more rural class of dwelling found expression in the erection of a new type of house. A daily service of coaches, running from the outlying parts to the centre of the metropolis, was inaugurated—the forerunners of the tube trains and motor omnibuses of to-day—and many a city merchant, professional man, and well-to-do tradesman, took advantage of the facilities of easy travel that these coaches offered to live at some distance from the scenes of his daily work.

Again, at this time it became the increasing custom of those who could afford it to spend some part of their leisure time either at a seaside town or at one of the spas. Bath and Tunbridge Wells had long enjoyed the favour of holiday-makers and those who for reasons of health or pleasure desired a change of scene and occupation.

The habit of taking an annual holiday at the seaside is of a slightly later date; but following the example of George III, who

Introduction

was ordered to Weymouth by his physicians, it quickly became fashionable amongst all ranks of society.

> Your prudent grandmammas, ye modern belles,
> Content with Bristol, Bath, and Tunbridge Wells,
> When health required it, would consent to roam,
> Else more attached to pleasures found at home;
> But now alike, gay widow, virgin, wife,
> Ingenious to diversify dull life,
> In coaches, chaises, caravans, and hoys,
> Fly to the coast for daily, nightly joys,
> And all impatient of dry land, agree
> With one consent to rush into the sea.
>
> COWPER—*Retirement*.

The result was that whole districts were given over to the holiday-makers, and what had been small fishing villages rapidly grew into pleasure towns of considerable magnitude. Margate, Ramsgate, Deal, Hastings, Brighton, Scarborough, Lowestoft, and innumerable others may be said to have owed their rise to prosperity to these causes. Jane Austen, in her novel "Persuasion," gives an interesting picture of a party of excursionists by the sea in the years immediately following the close of the Napoleonic wars. The town described is Lyme Regis, and the life led by its summer visitors does not appear to have been very different, allowing for the absence of cinemas, from that which may be enjoyed at any modern seaside resort to-day. "They were come too late in the year for any amusement or variety which Lyme as a public place might offer; the rooms were shut up, the lodgers almost all gone, scarcely any family but of the residents left, and, as there is nothing left to admire in the buildings themselves, the remarkable situation of the town, the principal street almost hanging in the water, the walk to the Cobb, skirting round the pleasant little bay, which in the season is animated with bathing-machines and company." A little further on there is a reference to the circulating library. All this would seem to suggest that very early in the nineteenth century the custom of paying an annual visit to the sea was firmly established amongst a considerable section of society. The buildings of these seaside towns—though, judging from the above, a little too modern for Miss Austen's taste—have a good deal of character and charm, and in many cases are quite distinct in type from the town or country residence.

The earliest are mostly remarkable for segmental bow windows carried up from the ground level to the top of the building. Many examples of this kind are to be found in the south-

Introduction

coast towns, and the illustration on Plate 22 of a house at Weymouth is a typical one, though the columns introduced at the ground-floor level give it a distinctive note of its own. Very often this bay extended to the full width of the room and afforded to the inmates a good view over the surrounding country. Afterwards a similar type of bay was employed, with the addition of verandahs and balconies such as are found in parts of Brighton and Hastings. Pelham Crescent, Hastings, is an interesting essay in this treatment. The roofs and delicate ironwork of the verandahs were often painted a bright shade of green, and the contrast this afforded against the white or light cream walls of smooth plaster was very gay, and gave a fitting expression to the pleasure-seeking nature of the town and its visitors.

An outside balcony with or without a verandah is an almost universal feature with the later seaside houses. It was felt that the views could be better and more healthily enjoyed in the open air, with the addition, if possible, of some shelter from the sun. The introduction of these balconies and verandahs was not without its effect on the more urban and rural houses, and we find these features in dwellings many miles from the sea.

The pair of houses illustrated on Plate 85 is a case in point. These were probably built in the early years of the nineteenth century, when the use of smooth stucco for the outside elevations had become very general. The beautiful iron balconies to the first-floor windows are very typical of the period, and are of a pattern frequently seen in the houses of the seaside towns, such as Hastings and Margate, which at this time were beginning to be fashionable holiday resorts. As town houses they are peculiarly interesting, suggesting as they do, in the freedom of their design, the summer experiences of an urban population. It is instructive to contrast with these the terrace of houses shown on Plate 17 from the same neighbourhood, which are more frankly suburban. They have neither the formality of the town, nor have they quite the freedom of the rural houses of the period. The view shows a collection of houses evidently erected by different owners, and designed with little relation to one another; but the harmony of style that prevails, so characteristic of the architecture of this time, is productive of an effect of repose which no mere formality of composition can give. The doorway to one of these houses is shown on Plate 18. The semicircular opening in the wall, filled in with delicate detail, was a favourite treatment for entrance doors

Introduction

employed by late-eighteenth-century architects. This particular example, with the slender columns and beautifully enriched transom, together with the graceful fanlight over, is very reminiscent of the American "colonial" work.

In reviewing these houses one is constantly tempted to make the analogy between them and the contemporary buildings in America. Whether the similarity in design to be observed in so many of them was the result of a reflex action on the work of the mother country by the colonials, or whether they were simply divergent though related branches of the earlier work in England, it is impossible exactly to determine. We know that communication with the colonies was regular, and except during the short period of the War of Independence unbroken, and that during this time there was a constant interchange of architectural ideas both in the form of books and by the personal visits of architects, and it is almost inconceivable that the distinctive work of the developed Georgian in America should have been without any influence on the designs of the English architects.

For instance, Surrey Lodge, Plate 5, at Denmark Hill, London, has much in common with a colonial house. The graceful Ionic columns with the tenderly moulded caps and enriched frieze to the entablature over, forming an ample and generous balcony to the ground-floor rooms, is strangely reminiscent of certain houses in the New England and Southern States, and many others might be cited as forming a similar comparison.

The spirit of the latter half of the eighteenth century was that of an urban civilization radiating its influence from the towns outwards towards the surrounding country. The larger towns, and in particular the capital, acted as magnets which attracted all those with any outstanding mental or social gifts. In an arresting passage one of the most penetratively critical modern writers * gives a vivid picture of the intellectual domination that London exercised at this time: "Imagine first the sort of life that was led in remote parts of Yorkshire or Somerset, towards the end of the eighteenth century, a stagnant rustic life with no ideas, and unquestioning in its obedience to authority, in which hardly anyone could read except the parson, and the parson's reading was not of a kind to stir a man's pulse. And next imagine the intellectual ferment which was then in progress in London or Paris; the philosophers, painters, historians, and men of science, the voices proclaiming that all men were equal, that the laws of England were unjust to the poor, that slavery was

---

* Professor Gilbert Murray in his "Euripides and his Age."

Introduction

a crime, and that monarchy was a false form of government, or that no action was morally wrong except what tended to produce human misery. Imagine then what would occur in the mind of a clever and high-thinking boy who was brought from the one society into the heart of the second, and made to realize that the battles and duties and prizes of life were tenfold more thrilling and important than he had ever dreamed." This condition of social life was not without its influence on the architecture of the time,* and this is the reason why so much of the best work is to be found in the houses of an urban or semi-urban character. The feeling for tradition was stronger in the country, which only by slow degrees absorbed the ideas of the town, more often than not content with tricking out some old house in the guise of the new; but this action of town on country was two-fold, for there was also the counteraction of the country on the town. As we have already seen, the populations of the towns were gradually extending outwards, and echoes of the country and seaside type of house are not infrequently met with in more urban centres.

Perhaps the foregoing can be better explained by a reference to the plates. For instance, the two houses at Cobham, in Surrey (see Plate 39), with their naïve, village-like simplicity, are still not entirely of the village, but own a distant relationship with the town. A close analysis reveals that the good effect of the whole is largely due to the proportion of windows to wall space and to their careful disposition. In each house they cluster round the entrance door, seeming to emphasize the individual dwelling, which at the same time forms one continuous composition with its neighbour. They are sufficiently elegant in design (the keynote of which is to be found in the detail of the doors) to suggest the culture of the city imposing itself on the quiet and harmonious life of the countryside.

Again, taking another pair of houses, this time in Quarry Street, Guildford (see Plate 38), where the design denotes the more reserved but friendly nature of the country town, and the absence

---

* Uppercross was a moderate-sized village, which a few years back had been completely in the old English style; containing only two houses superior in appearance to those of the yeoman and labourer—the mansion of the squire with its high walls, great gates, and old trees, substantial and unmodernized, and the compact tight parsonage enclosed in its own neat garden, with a vine and a pear-tree trained round its casements; but upon the marriage of the young squire, it had received the improvement of a farm-house elevated into a cottage for his residence; and Uppercross Cottage with its verandah, French windows, and other prettinesses was quite as likely to catch the traveller's eye, as the more consistent and considerable aspect of the Great House, about a quarter of a mile farther on.—JANE AUSTEN.

Introduction

of the forecourt railing, an almost inevitable adjunct to a similar type of house in town, implies the difference between the trustfulness of the rural and the suspiciousness of the urban citizen. In general, these two different groups of houses conform more closely to the earlier and more traditional style, and the comparison between them and those at Kennington (see Plates 17 and 85) is very striking.

The distinguishing trait of most of these Late Georgian houses is a sense of order and proportion; nothing has been left to chance, all has been considered even to the minutest detail; but together with all this carefully concealed study there is a spontaneity about them and a freshness of conception. There is a wonderful variety in their design, evidencing a wealth of invention and a fertility of imagination which is only possible when the canons and fundamentals of an art are frankly accepted. In the limitations of his style the artist has found true freedom for his efforts, which for want of definite guiding principles of recognized convention might all too easily have been wasted in a vain striving after a false originality, and his time frittered away in the pursuit of a vain and elusive interest. In the quiet restraint and dignity of their setting these homes of a bygone generation are expressive of a very high form of civilization. There is a beautiful propriety about them which, with their air of distinction, reveals them to be the residences of a well-bred and cultured people. They have a shy beauty, an atmosphere, as it were, of sunny charm; in the refinement of their details and in the balance of their parts they are indicative of a well-ordered and cheerful community which has found the happiest inspiration in the building of its homes. They are the product of a different age from that in which we live—of an age that had some regard for the forms and amenities of social intercourse, a time of leisure and of manners, but a period not without its limitations.

The sense of tradition, the resultant sum of those subtle influences that form and mould the taste—so difficult to determine and classify, but of the very essence of life—is felt as some invisible chain of gold upon which time has threaded these smaller houses, representing as they do a continuous development from the days of that inspired innovator Inigo Jones, the first and foremost of our Classic builders. In their development and frequent deviations they picture the changing outlook and customs of their possessors; but new ideas and features are absorbed by a natural process, and there is a continuity of style that embraces and enfolds them all. To be able to determine cause from effect in architecture is to

Introduction

possess the keynote of style, the attempt to possess which by a mere study of results, without some understanding of the manners and customs of the people that produced them, in the realization of our own artistic efforts can at best result only in some dexterous form of copyism, devoid of all vital and living impulses. The models of the past should serve rather for inspiration and emulation, instead of what has all too frequently happened with so many of our enthusiastic discoverers—as examples to be imitated with painstaking, not to say pain-giving, exactitude. It was not until the advent of the Greek revival, which laid so cold a hand on our throbbing and pulsating domestic art, with its imposition of the Greek orders, tending to convert the home into the diminutive ghost of some ancient temple, that the tradition finally died; though even then there was a persistence of the original stock strong enough for a time to subordinate the Greek elements to its purpose, and to limit strictly the application of the orders to such subsidiary features as doors and porticoes.

The influence of the leading architects on the smaller works of their day, even when not directly carried out by them, is plainly discernible. Of the earlier architects who in point of time are just outside the limits of our survey, William Kent and Isaac Ware are probably the most important. Mr. Reginald Blomfield, in criticizing Kent's buildings, states: "They are severely, almost pedantically, simple; their proportions are good, and Kent avoided the heavy-handed touch which spoilt the work of some of his contemporaries."* And it is with just these qualities of proportion and lightness of touch that Kent paved the way for Robert Adam and the later men. The influence of Isaac Ware was of a two-fold nature, which he exerted by precept in his numerous publications, and by practice in the many buildings that he carried out both in London and the country. But Ware's designs belong rather to the older than the newer school; he is not so revolutionary as Kent, and may perhaps be said to have been the leader which Sir William Chambers and Sir Robert Taylor, those brilliant competitors of the brothers Adam, followed. His book, published in 1756, which he called "A Complete Body of Architecture," had a great influence on both contemporary and later designers; and in spite of Ware's innate conservatism, his work and designs show signs of the coming manner.

---

* "A Short History of the Renaissance in England," by Reginald Blomfield.

Introduction

About 1760 Robert Adam and his brother established themselves in practice, and to them must be ascribed the dominating influence in Domestic Architecture for the next thirty years. Though in the arrangement and disposition of their masses they did not depart widely from the Palladianism of the early architects, in the treatment of the parts of their buildings they achieved a marked originality; they may be described as having domesticated the "Classic," and it is in the details of their work that they are most happily remembered. It was on the entrance door, the fanlight, the ceiling, and the fireplace that they lavished their special gifts, with the result that they have left us a series of models which for their particular purpose cannot be bettered. Apart from the interest in the designs, we cannot be indifferent to the excellence of the craftsmanship displayed in their executed work. Architect and artisan would appear to have worked in complete accord the one with the other, the conceptions of the former being carried out with faultless execution by the latter.

The earlier Georgian house, with its wide window-frames set in an outside reveal, with heavily moulded sashes and glazing-bars, the heavy mutule cornice supporting a deep, red-tiled roof which frequently contained attics with dormers, now gave place to a more refined and formal type, with slighter and more carefully considered mouldings, roofs of a flatter pitch, and with windows set in an inside reveal. The treatment of the window is often a good but not infallible clue to the date of the building.

As early as 1730 we find instances of the window-frame set back four and a half inches from the face of a wall, and contained in a four and a half inch brick rebate. But by 1750, or 1760 at latest, this treatment of window-frames had become general, though there was a transitional period when the frame was set back four and a half inches from the wall-face, but was contained in a two and a quarter inch reveal, with frequently the addition of a moulded architrave on the outside, against the side of the brick opening and the frame. The glazing-bars after 1750 were usually of a much smaller section, though the use of the stouter bars, and even of frames set on the face of the wall in an outside reveal as in the earlier examples, is found in certain country districts quite late in the eighteenth century. Brick was still generally employed for elevations in the smaller houses when considerations of cost did not permit of stone; but the brickwork was of a neater kind than formerly, the proportion of void to solid received greater study than before, the use of brown or yellow bricks for

Introduction

the whole façade now became general, and slate as a roofing material seems to have been preferred to tiles.

If Robert Adam exerted a great influence on the external designs of the houses of his day, he was responsible in perhaps a greater degree for radical alterations in the plans. He was extremely successful in the creation of vistas and in the arrangement of his rooms *en suite;* he also to a greater extent than formerly designed apartments of a circular or oval shape; and it is extremely instructive to compare his system of planning with that of the contemporary French architects, with whose work he was without doubt well acquainted. This use of circular and oval forms was carried on by his successors in the profession, and there are examples of comparatively small houses in which rooms of this shape are to be found. Stone House, Lewisham (see Plate 20), has a very fine circular drawing-room immediately behind the portico to the garden front.

One result of the more formal and comprehensive treatment of design by the late eighteenth-century architects was the increasing tendency to group numbers of houses together in one elevation wherever circumstances gave them an opportunity for so doing.

The Paragon at Blackheath (see Plates 71, 72), built in the closing years of the eighteenth century, shows what a striking effect can be obtained when series of houses of moderate size are unified under one scheme. The treatment of the different blocks linked up with the Doric arcades is most original, preserving as it does the continuity of the design, whilst indicating the individuality of the separate houses. The detail throughout, though delicate in execution, is extremely masculine and direct. The Paragon was originally built with the idea of providing accommodation for naval officers stationed at Greenwich, or for those who had retired from the service; and this, no doubt, was partially responsible for the suggestion of a uniform treatment for their residences.

The Adam brothers had many followers both in this country and America; and though in the list of their projected or executed works there are very few small houses which are known to have been designed by them, there are innumerable examples throughout Scotland and England which may be said to be the work of their school.

Garrick's Villa, which Robert Adam built for the celebrated actor at Hampton-on-Thames (see Plate 16), is an example of the smaller houses designed by the Adams. The riverside

Introduction

house with its beautifully enriched portico is the forerunner of many similar houses built both in this country and the United States, and may be said to have had a notable influence on the development of colonial architecture.

Reference has already been made to Sir William Chambers and Sir Robert Taylor, who with James Paine and Carr of York are some of the best known of their contemporaries.

Chambers was chiefly concerned with buildings of a public character, and the few houses that he designed, like those of Carr of York, and Taylor, are examples of a refined Palladianism. A glance at the two houses by Sir Robert Taylor (Plate 31 and Plate 32) will perhaps better explain this phase. Asgill House, Richmond, a house in grey stone, is a fine example of a small residence treated in a broad and generous manner, and has an air of patrician distinction. Such a feature as a semi-octagonal bay is always an extremely difficult thing to manage in a Classic building, and the solution afforded by this design, in which the bay is the dominant feature of the elevation, embracing some of the principal apartments, is very successful. Both this house and Thorncroft Manor, Leatherhead, built in 1772, are dignified compositions produced out of the simplest elements, but without the originality, and in a certain measure without the charm, of the Adam house; they follow much more closely on the traditional lines of the older work, and are of a more consistent aspect.

From now onwards there may be said to have been two traditions which were followed, often indiscriminately, by the succeeding builders; that of the Adam brothers, and that of the late Palladian group, the one frequently reacting on the other, and vice versa. The house on Holywell Hill, St. Albans (Plate 3), built in 1785, and the Brown House at Reigate (Frontispiece and Plate 4), built in 1784, may be said to owe their inspiration to these two main schools of design, with perhaps a hint in the one at Reigate of an even earlier Georgian prototype. Contemporary with these two main streams of design there was a third current or backwater of much smaller dimensions owing its origin to the "Gothic" manner of Horace Walpole and Batty Langley. When Walpole, that whimsical connoisseur, essayed to build that amazing villa of his at Strawberry Hill, Twickenham, which was started in 1750 and finished in 1776, he threw aside the Classic models and sought inspiration in the buildings of the Middle Ages.

Introduction

The first stirrings of the Romantic movement were in the air, and after years of long neglect to pretend to an admiration and understanding of the cathedrals and abbeys became the fashion. Whether this enterprising patron of the arts was really moved by a genuine love of these older buildings, and endeavoured in his own house to emulate them, or was simply moved by a perverse desire to produce something different from his neighbours, is an open question. Batty Langley, who lived during the first half of the eighteenth century, must bear with Walpole the responsibility for the introduction of this new mode.

Langley was an indefatigable writer, and his numerous publications were not without some influence on the succeeding generation of architects. He it was who attempted to arrange Gothic architecture under five orders, and his failure here marks the limitation of his influence. The authority of the prevailing Classic was too strong for him and his followers to emancipate themselves completely; and the immediate effect, as far as building was concerned, was confined to the introduction of a certain Gothic feeling in such secondary motifs as doors and windows. The house in Well Walk, Hampstead (Plate 24), dating from about the middle of the eighteenth century, is an interesting instance of the "Gothic" of that time. This captivating little house in the disposition of its parts, as also the treatment of its detail, is fundamentally classical, and the transmuted Gothic simply serves to give it a gay and vivid interest. The porch, with its "Gothic Order" already referred to, the large bay on the first floor and window above, all seem to have been designed by a Georgian architect seeking pleasant adventure in the Gothic field. But this so-called Gothic school had very little real influence on the main tendencies of design, and to-day it is chiefly remembered through a certain criss-cross use of glazing bars in sash windows, a form of window largely used by the architects of the latter end of the eighteenth century, both in this country and America.

The Adam tradition was carried on by the Wyatts, Bonomi, and Thomas Leverton, and the houses built by these architects are chiefly remarkable for the use that is made of stucco as a material for the treatment of façades.

As introduced by the brothers Adam, Liardet's stucco and Coade's patent stone were generally employed on the elevations for the architectural embellishments only; but, as has been said, stucco was afterwards used for the complete clothing of a house, and, when not abused, this treatment, which always enables a

Introduction

building by a coat of paint to renew its youthful appearance, has much to recommend it.

The house in Bell Street, Henley (Plate 78), with the interesting treatment of a ground-floor bay and the widely projecting eaves supported on slight and well-shaped brackets, so characteristic of the designs of this group, and "Hollydale," Keston Common (Plate 15), are good examples of these stuccoed houses. But a new element in house design was now imminent.

In 1762 Stuart and Revett published their "Athenian Antiquities," and the era of the Greek revival had begun. Fortunately financial considerations in the main kept our smaller houses free of these great columniated fronts which apparently delighted the builders of the greater mansions in the closing years of the eighteenth and early part of the nineteenth century; but the smaller dwellings unmistakably reflect the new-found enthusiasms of the time. Drayton House, St. Margarets, Middlesex (Plate 99), the house at Herne Hill (Plate 91), and the house at Blackheath (Plate 73), illustrate this tendency, and one and all bear witness to the efforts of the well-meaning but heavy-handed archæologist. These houses have an interest of their own, but the interest is in what they suggest rather than what they actually are; they belong both to the immediate and the remote past, and they are at the same time aged and immature, without either the vigour of middle-life or the engaging candour of youth.

Perhaps it is hardly fair to blame the creators of these houses for the mistakes common to their age and to that renewed enthusiasm for the classics which the archæologists had brought about. Neither would it be fair to these same archæologists to dismiss them with a few contemptuous sentences, for it is only to-day that we are reaping the harvest of their careful sowing, and it only needs a rapid glance at the work of the French students at Rome to see what treasures of design have been restored to us from the past. But the immediate effect of all this learning on the domestic architecture of this country was disastrous, and it remained for the Gothic revivalists to rescue it from the hands of the pedants.

This brief review might fittingly close with a few words on John Nash. Nash was a pupil of Sir Robert Taylor, and in his work we still see some slight remaining influence of the Palladianism of his master combined with the new "Greek" and "Roman" of his time, with here and there an echo of the Adam tradition.

The position of Nash in the history of English architecture is almost a unique one. He, together with his predecessors, Robert Adam and the Woods of Bath, laid the foundations of

Introduction

modern town-planning in its more monumental aspects, as applied to the treatment of streets and street façades. Nash was a great believer in the use of smooth stucco for the fronts of his buildings, and indeed scarcely ever employed any other material for this purpose. Even in the smallest of his works, as well as in his more ambitious undertakings, he aimed at a subjection of detail to general harmony, and everything was considered from the standpoint of total effect. His work, though at times somewhat theatrical in its setting, is always expressive of reticence and refinement—no mean qualities—and is not wanting in a certain masculine vigour which saves it from any charge of insipidity. But he was practically the last of the architects of the older school; the flame of the Georgian tradition, which had burnt so brightly for close upon one hundred years, finally went out, and the age of the revivals had arrived. The Greek revival was followed by the Roman, the Roman by the Italian, the Italian by the Gothic, and the cycle has been continued down to our own day, with the result, possibly, of enlarging the boundaries of our sympathies, the necessary prelude to some new setting of the stage. Whether we shall ever again have a continuous tradition remains for future generations to determine. But it is difficult to conceive of any such tradition which shall be built up without any knowledge or understanding of the past, and in such a study of architectural history the subject of these lesser houses might have some place. In many districts where the clamant demands of an ever-growing population have to be quickly satisfied, these humble buildings, without any particular claim to such architectural or historical interest as might save some greater and more important building, are rapidly passing away; and it was the idea of preserving some record of the more interesting of these houses that eventually led to the production of this book.

Plate 1

ASHLEY HOUSE, EPSOM.

ASHLEY HOUSE, EPSOM: PORCH.

HOUSE ON HOLYWELL HILL, ST. ALBANS.

BROWN HOUSE, REIGATE: GARDEN FRONT.

Plate 5

General View from Roadway

Detail of Portico.

SURREY LODGE, DENMARK HILL, LONDON, S.E.

Plate 6

HOUSES IN OWEN STREET, HEREFORD.

Photo by W. H. Bustin.

SHOP IN OWEN STREET, HEREFORD.

Plate 7

DOORWAY IN OWEN STREET, HEREFORD.

Photo by W. H. Bustin.

DOORWAY TO CHANDOS HOUSE, HEREFORD.

WANTLEY MANOR, HENFIELD, SUSSEX.

Plate 9

HOUSE AT HENFIELD, SUSSEX.

Plate 10

HOUSES IN DOYLE ROAD, ST. PETER PORT, GUERNSEY.

Plate 11

HOUSE IN DOYLE ROAD, ST. PETER PORT, GUERNSEY: GARDEN FRONT.

HOUSE ON THE SAUMAREZ ROAD, GUERNSEY.

Plate 13

NORTHFIELD HOUSE, HENLEY.

"THE WICK," RICHMOND HILL, SURREY.

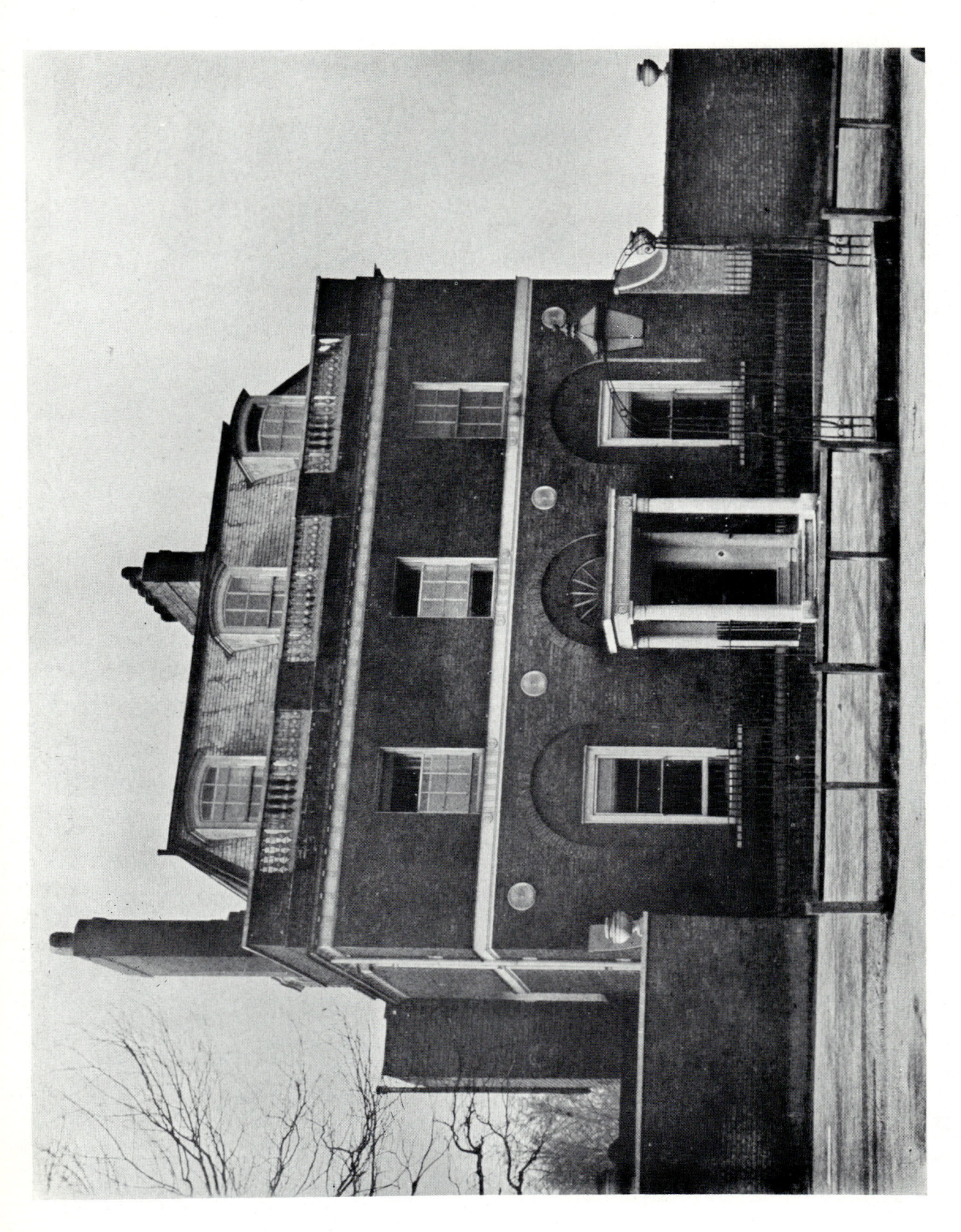

"HOLLYDALE," KESTON, KENT.

GARRICK VILLA. HAMPTON-ON-THAMES.

HOUSES ON KENNINGTON GREEN, LONDON, S.E.

DOORWAY, KENNINGTON GREEN, LONDON, S.E.

Plate 19

DOORWAY AND BALCONY, STAFFORD HOUSE, UPPER KENNINGTON LANE, LONDON, S.E.

STONE HOUSE, LEWISHAM, LONDON, S.E.

THE GRANGE, ST. PETER'S STREET, ST. ALBANS.

PORCH, STONE HOUSE, LEWISHAM, LONDON, S.E.

HOUSE ON THE PARADE, WEYMOUTH.

Plate 22

HOUSES IN CASTLE STREET, HEREFORD.

TERRACE OF HOUSES IN WIDMARSH STREET, HEREFORD.

Photo by W. H. Bustin.

HOUSE IN WELL WALK, HAMPSTEAD, N.W.

KENT HOUSE, THE MALL, HAMMERSMITH

STRAWBERRY HOUSE, THE MALL, CHISWICK.

Kennington Road, S.E. The Mall, Chiswick, W.

TWO LONDON DOORWAYS.

Plate 28

THE VICARAGE, 22 LOWER MALL, HAMMERSMITH.

Plate 29

BRAMPTON HOUSE, CHURCH STREET, CHISWICK.

Plate 30

LINDEN HOUSE, THE MALL, HAMMERSMITH, LONDON.

Plate 31

ASGILL HOUSE, RICHMOND, SURREY.

Plate 32

THORNCROFT MANOR LEATHERHEAD, SURREY.

Plate 33

TOLL HOUSE, HENLEY.

PORTICO IN RUSKIN PARK, DENMARK HILL, LONDON.
(A Fragment of Captain Wilson's House.)

DOORWAY, ANCASTER HOUSE, RICHMOND HILL, SURREY.

Plate 35

DOORWAY, THE GREEN, RICHMOND, SURREY.

DOORWAY, QUARRY STREET, GUILDFORD.

"WOODBINE COTTAGE," PETERSHAM, SURREY.

Plate 37

Photo by Francis R. Taylor.

HOUSES IN CHISWICK LANE, LONDON, W.

PAIR OF HOUSES, QUARRY STREET, GUILDFORD.

Plate 39

PAIR OF HOUSES AT COBHAM, SURREY.

Plate 40

FARM-HOUSE AT COBHAM, SURREY.

Plate 41

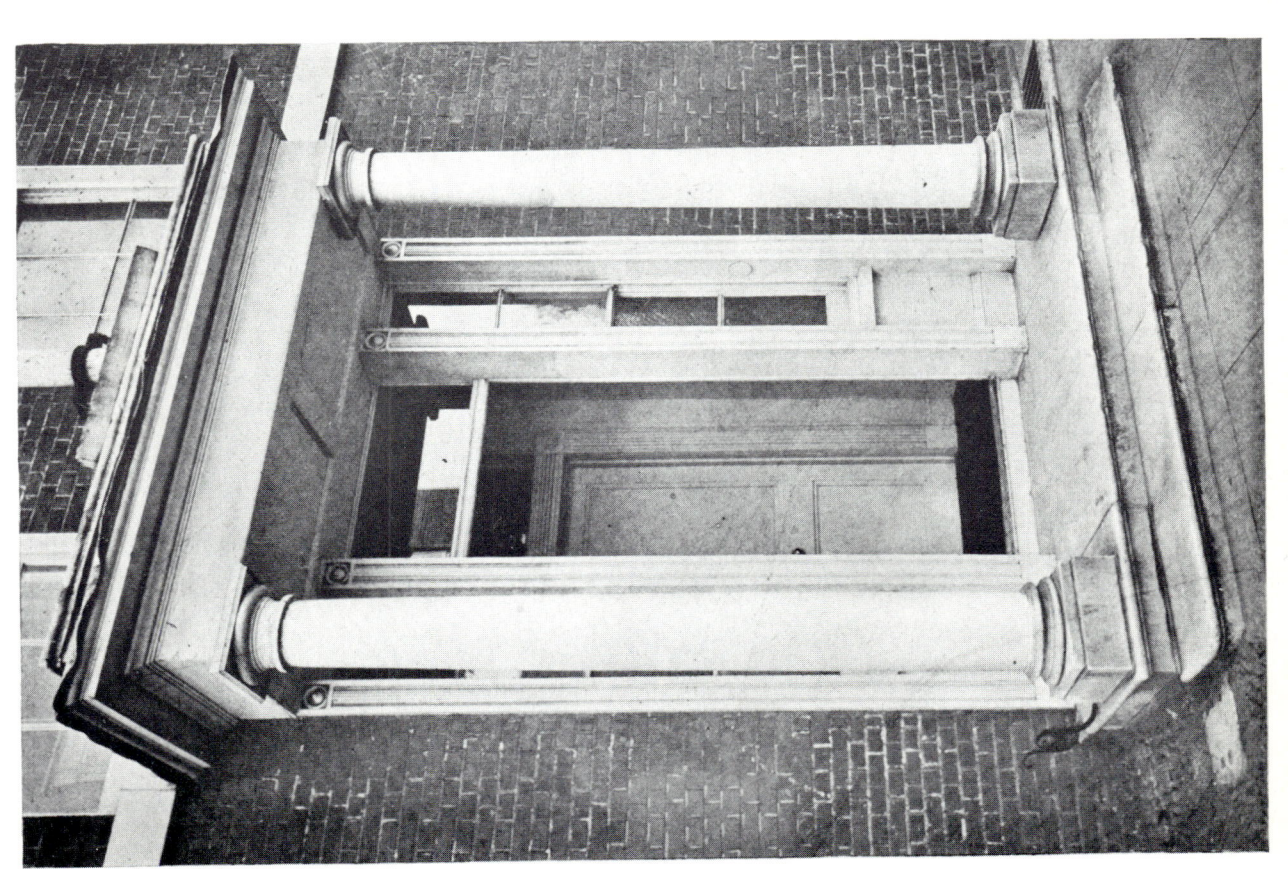

DOORWAY IN ST. PETER'S STREET, ST. ALBANS.

DOORWAY IN HIGH STREET, MARLOW.

Plate 42

HOUSE AT COBHAM, SURREY.

Plate 43

"THE RUNNING HORSES" INN, MICKLEHAM, SURREY.

Plate 44

HOUSES IN BROAD STREET, STAMFORD.

Plate 45

THE WHITE LION HOTEL, COBHAM, SURREY.

Plate 46

WEATHERBOARDED HOUSE AT ASHTEAD, SURREY.

Plate 47

WEATHERBOARDED COTTAGES AT CAPEL, SURREY.

Plate 48

WEATHERBOARDED COTTAGES IN BARROW ROAD, STREATHAM.

WEATHERBOARDED COTTAGES AT ST. ALBANS.

Plate 49

HOUSE AT HAMPSTEAD.

ELM HOUSE, HENLEY.

Plate 50

TWO HOUSES IN THE HIGH STREET, MARLOW.

Plate 51

HOUSES FACING ALFRED SQUARE, DEAL.

Photo by Francis R. Taylor.

COTTAGES IN FISHPOOL STREET, ST. ALBANS

COTTAGES IN SANDRIDGE ROAD, ST. ALBANS.

RIVER-HOUSE TO SYON HOUSE, ISLEWORTH.

DETAIL OF ENTRANCE TO HOUSE IN CAMBERWELL ROAD, LONDON, S.E.

VERANDAH ON HOUSES, CROSS KEYS ESTATE, ST. ALBANS.

Plate 55

PORCH, BLACKHEATH HILL, LONDON, S.E.

DOORWAY, LOWER KENNINGTON LANE, LONDON, S.E.

HOUSE AT ESHER, SURREY.

No. 6 SOUTHWOOD LANE, HIGHGATE, LONDON, N.

Forbes House.

Ensleigh Lodge.

TWO HOUSES ON HAM COMMON, SURREY.

LANGHAM HOUSE, HAM, SURREY.

HOUSE IN ST. PETER'S STREET, ST. ALBANS.

Plate 60

PORCH TO SOUTHWOOD HOUSE, HIGHGATE, LONDON.

HOUSE ON THE TERRACE, BARNES.

HOUSE ON THE TERRACE, BARNES.

PORCH, "THE LIMES," KINGSTON-ON-THAMES.

MILBOURNE HOUSE, BARNES.

Plate 66

PORCH TO HOUSE IN CHURCH ROW, HAMPSTEAD

COTTAGES IN SOUTHWOOD LANE, HAMPSTEAD

Plate 67

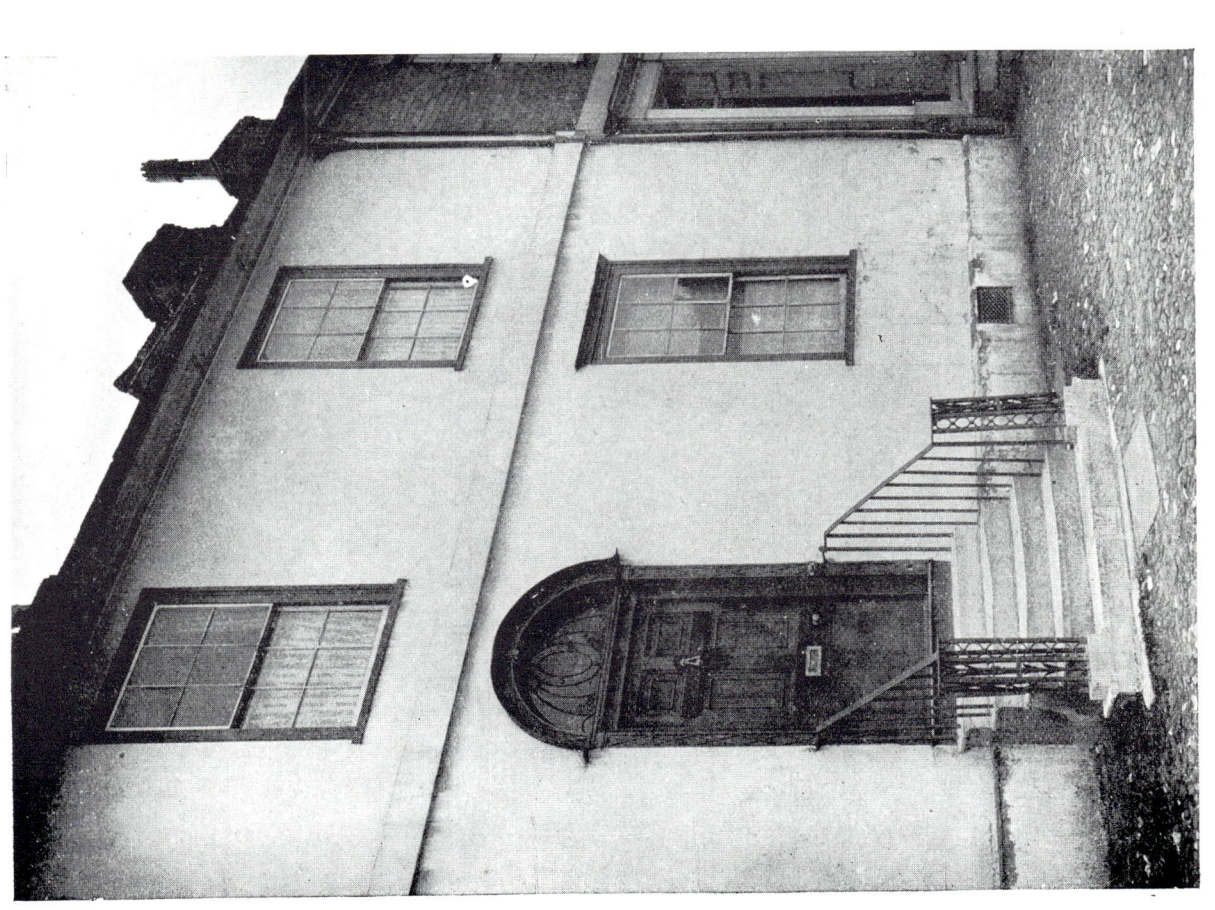

COTTAGES AT STOKESLEY, YORKSHIRE.

HOUSE AT THAXTED, ESSEX.

COUNCIL HOUSE, BARNES.

Plate 69

TERRACE ON RICHMOND HILL.

Plate 70

At Dorking.

At Leatherhead.

TWO TRELLIS PORCHES.

Plate 71

THE PARAGON, BLACKHEATH, LONDON, S E

THE PARAGON, BLACKHEATH, LONDON, S.E.: DETAIL OF WING.

Plate 73

TWO HOUSES AT BLACKHEATH, LONDON, S.E.

Plate 74

Pond Lane, Lower Clapton

At Merton, Surrey.

SOME WEATHER-BOARDED COTTAGES.

Plate 75

HOUSE AT TRURO.

HOUSE ON CHAMPION HILL, LONDON, S.E.

Plate 76

Plate 77

DURLSTONE MANOR, CHAMPION HILL, LONDON, S.E.

Plate 78

HOUSE IN BELL STREET, HENLEY.

THE ELMS, EPSOM.

Plate 80

HOUSE AT HORSHAM, SURREY.

Plate 81

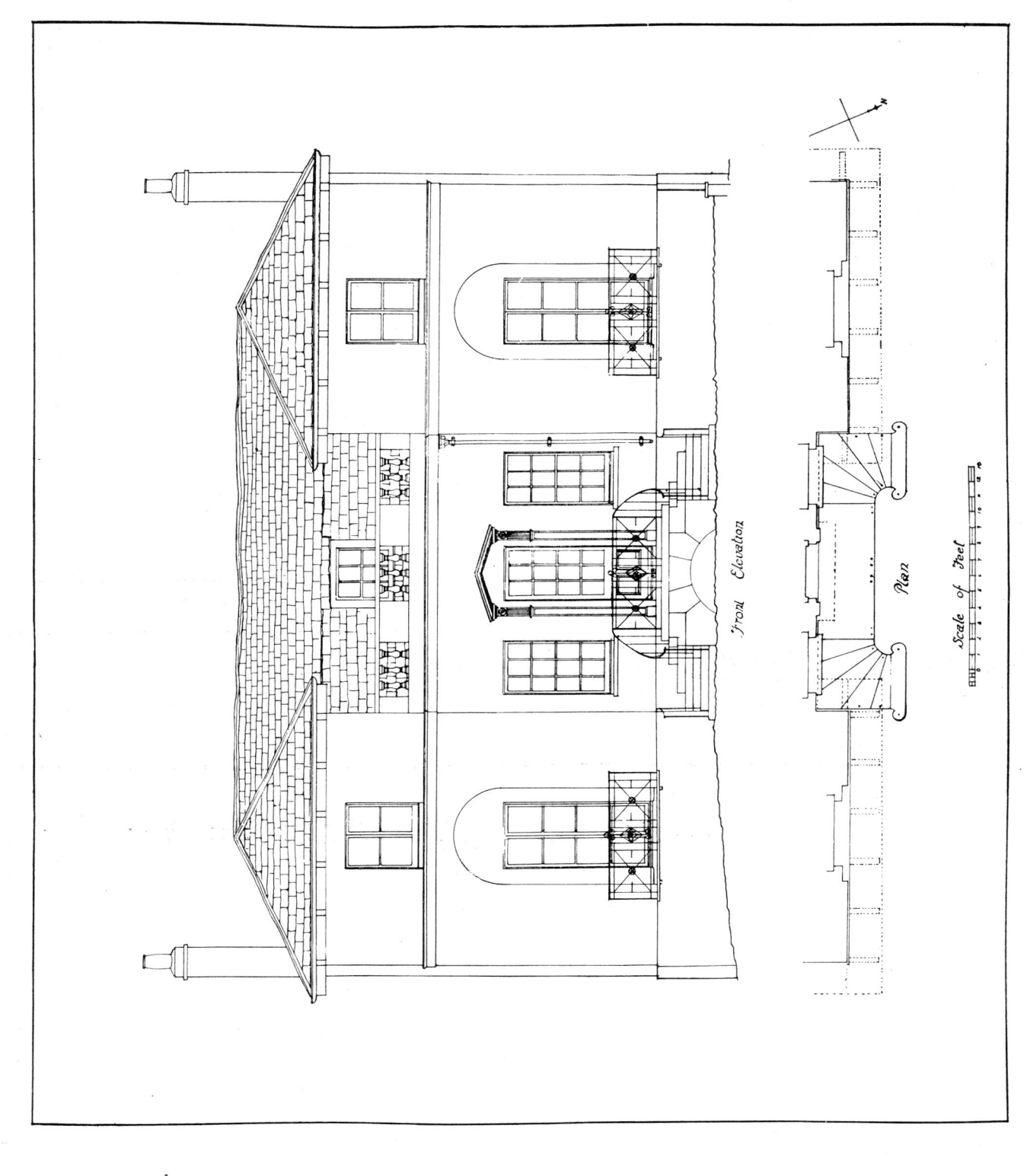

Front Elevation

Plan

Scale of Feet

HOUSE AT KENNINGTON OVAL, LONDON, S.E. (NOW DEMOLISHED).

Plate 82

SHOP AT DORKING, SURREY.

Plate 83

SHOP IN WIDMARSH STREET, HEREFORD.

Photo by W. H. Bustin

SHOP NEAR CATHEDRAL, HEREFORD.

Plate 84

HOUSE IN HIGH STREET, MARLOW

HOUSE AT STAR CROSS, DEVONSHIRE.

Plate 85

TWO HOUSES IN KENNINGTON ROAD, LONDON, S.E.

Plate 86

DOCTOR'S HOUSE, NEW CROSS, LONDON, S.E.

Plate 87

CEDAR LODGE, BLACKHEATH, LONDON, S.E.

OFFICE, BURY STREET, BLOOMSBURY, LONDON, W.

Plate 88

TERRACE ON RICHMOND HILL.

TERRACE IN SHEEN LANE, MORTLAKE.

Plate 89

HURST COTTAGE, HAMPTON, MIDDLESEX.

HOUSE AT ST. MARGARET'S, MIDDLESEX.

HOUSE AT ST. ALBANS.

Plate 91

HOUSE AT HERNE HILL.

PAIR OF HOUSES IN WATER LANE, BRIXTON.

Plate 92

COTTAGES AT GIGGSHILL GREEN, NEAR ESHER, SURREY.

Plate 93

HOUSE ON THE HAGLEY ROAD, BIRMINGHAM.

Plate 94

HALNAKER LODGE, COLDHARBOUR LANE, BRIXTON, LONDON, S.W.

Plate 95

"OAKFIELD," DULWICH VILLAGE.

Plate 96

MORDEN LODGE, MORDEN, SURREY.

Plate 97

Photo by A. Honey

BERKELEY HOUSE, CORPORATION STREET, ROCHESTER.

Plate 98

SHOPS IN WOBURN PLACE, LONDON, W.C.

DRAYTON HOUSE, ST. MARGARET'S, MIDDLESEX.

Plate 100

DOORWAY TO HOUSE AT HAMPTON, MIDDLESEX.

DOORWAY IN HIGH STREET, ROCHFORD, ESSEX.

DOORWAY TO CONNAUGHT HOUSE, ROCHFORD, ESSEX.

DOORWAY IN HIGH STREET, ROCHFORD, ESSEX.

II. INTERIORS AND DETAILS

Including fifty photographs by the late F. R. Yerbury, Hon. A.R.I.B.A.

LIST OF PLATES

Frontispiece		A Vase, Pitzhanger Manor, Ealing.
		Entrance Hall, No. 1 Bedford Square.
Plate	1.	Entrance Hall, Mottram Hall, Cheshire.
,,	2.	Staircase, Walpole House, Chiswick Mall.
,,	3.	Entrance, No. 35 Bedford Square.
		Entrance, Pitzhanger Manor, Ealing.
,,	4.	Entrance Hall, Gray Court, Ham.
		Entrance Hall, Kent House, The Mall, Hammersmith.
,,	5.	Staircase, "Oare," Pewsey, Wilts.
,,	6.	"Oare," Pewsey, Wilts.
,,	7.	Entrance Hall, No. 1 Bedford Square.
,,	8.	The Staircase, No. 1 Bedford Square.
,,	9.	Dining-room, No. 1 Bedford Square.
,,	10.	Dining-room, No. 1 Bedford Square.
,,	11.	A Chimneypiece in No. 1 Bedford Square.
,,	12.	Drawing-room, No. 1 Bedford Square.
,,	13.	Two Doorways at Kenwood, Hampstead.
,,	14.	Dining-room Doorway, Ely House, Dover Street, London. Sir Robert Taylor, Architect.
,,	15.	Staircase Hall, Ely House, Dover Street, London, W.
,,	16.	No. 21 Berners Street, W.
,,	17.	Doorway in No. 21 Berners Street, London.
,,	18.	Doorway at Harewood House, Hanover Square, London (Now Demolished).
,,	19.	Staircase, East Cliff House, Hastings.
,,	20.	No. 2 Bedford Square.
,,	21.	Drawing-room, No. 13 Bedford Square.
,,	22.	Carved Wood Chimneypiece (Now in the Victoria and Albert Museum).
,,	23.	Chimneypiece from an Old House in Canonbury Place, London.
,,	24.	End Bay of Drawing-room, Stone House, Lewisham.
,,	25.	Drawing-room, Stone House, Lewisham.
,,	26.	Asgill House, Richmond.
,,	27.	A Doorway, Asgill House, Richmond.
,,	28.	Asgill House, Richmond.
,,	29.	Bedroom in Asgill House, Richmond.
,,	30.	Fireplace at Asgill House, Richmond.
,,	31.	Mantelpiece in a House at Sheen, near Richmond, Surrey.
,,	32.	Fireplace in Walpole House, Chiswick Mall.
,,	33.	Fireplace in Kent House, Hammersmith Mall.
,,	34.	Archway on First Floor, No. 91 Cheyne Walk, Chelsea.
		Detail of Staircase, Gray Court, Ham.
,,	35.	Window in the Premises of Gill & Reigate, Ltd., The Soho Galleries.
		Fireplace from No. 51 Lincoln's Inn Fields.
,,	36.	The Large Smoking-room, Brooks's Club House, London.
,,	37.	The Saloon, Boodle's Club House, London.
,,	38.	Fireplaces in No. 7 Great George Street, Bristol.
,,	39.	Kelmscott House, Hammersmith Mall. Fireplace in Dining-room.
,,	40.	Chimneypiece from a House in Hatton Garden, London.
,,	41.	Carved Pine Fireplace, Formerly in a House in Edinburgh.
,,	42.	Pitzhanger Manor, Ealing.
,,	43.	Staircase, Pitzhanger Manor, Ealing.
,,	44.	Pitzhanger Manor, Ealing.
,,	45.	Ceiling, Belvedere House, Dublin.
		St. Stephen's Club, Dublin, Detail of Ceiling.
,,	46.	Ceiling at Kent House, Hammersmith.
		Ceiling at No. 2 Bedford Square.
,,	47.	Two London Chimneypieces of Marble.
,,	48.	Ceiling, No. 3 Adelphi Terrace, London. Robert Adam, Architect.
,,	49.	Central Bay of Coffee-room Ceiling, St. James's Club, London.
,,	50.	Details of Friezes at No. 35 Bedford Square.
,,	51.	Detail of a Late Eighteenth Century Bookcase.
,,	52.	Ceiling from No. 65 Lincoln's Inn Fields.
		Ceiling from No. 51 Lincoln's Inn Fields.
,,	53.	The Oval Staircase Hall in the Old War Office, Pall Mall, London (Now Demolished). Sir John Soane, Architect.
,,	54.	Doorcase from No. 29 Great George Street, Westminster (Now in the Victoria and Albert Museum, South Kensington).

List of Plates

Plate 55. Plaster Overmantel from No. 25 Parliament Street, Westminster (now in the Victoria and Albert Museum).
,, 56. Plaster Medallion from No. 29 Great George Street, Westminster.
,, 57. Catherine Lodge, Trafalgar Square, Chelsea. View of Staircase.
,, 58. Pitzhanger Manor, Ealing : Detail of Entrance Front. Detail of Entrance Arch.
,, 59. Garden Details at Pitzhanger House, Ealing.
,, 60. Entrance to the Manor House, Ham.

Forty Measured Drawings by J. D. M. Harvey

,, 61. Weather-boarded House, Carshalton, Surrey: Elevation and Details.
,, 62. Weather-boarded Cottages, Barrow Road, Streatham, London: Elevation and Details.
,, 63. Porch, Ashley House, Epsom, Surrey: Elevation, Section, and Details.
,, 64. Porch, Montrose House, Petersham, Surrey: Elevation, Section, and Details.
,, 65. The Paragon, Blackheath, London: Key Plan and Elevation. Elevation of one Block with Porter's Lodge.
,, 66. Fireplace at No. 5, The Paragon, Blackheath, London: Elevation, Section, and Details.
,, 67. The Colonnade House and The Paragon, Blackheath: Details.
,, 68. Colonnade House, Blackheath, London, S.E.: Elevation.
,, 69. Surrey Lodge, Denmark Hill, London, S.E.: Elevation.
,, 70. Surrey Lodge, Denmark Hill, London, S.E.: Details.
,, 71. House in Well Walk, Hampstead, London: Plan, Section, and Elevation of Entrance Front.
,, 72. The River House, Syon House, Isleworth: Plan and Elevation.
,, 73. The River House, Syon House, Isleworth: Section and Details.
,, 74. Porch, Southwood House, Highgate, London, N.: Elevation, Section, and Details.
,, 75. Porch, Ancaster House, Richmond: Elevation and Details.
,, 76. Trellis Porch, "The Limes," Kingston-on-Thames: Plan, Section, Elevation, and Details.
,, 77. Doorway and Balcony, Upper Kennington Lane, London, S.E.: Elevation and Details.
,, 78. Fireplace from a House in Great St. Helens, London, E.C. (Now in the Victoria and Albert Museum): Elevation and Details.
,, 79. Fireplace in the Victoria and Albert Museum, South Kensington, London: Elevation and Details.
,, 80. Stone House, Lewisham, London, S.E.: Fireplace and other Details.
,, 81. Stone House, Lewisham, London, S.E.: Elevation, Plan, and Details.
,, 82. Stone House, Lewisham, London, S.E.: The Drawing-room: Plan, Section, and Details.
,, 83. Kent House, Lower Mall, Hammersmith, London, W.: Elevation of Entrance Front.
,, 84. Kent House, Hammersmith, London, W.: Iron Railings to Forecourt, Elevations and Details.
,, 85. No. 71 Bell Street, Henley: Elevation and Details.
,, 86. "The Wick," Richmond, Surrey: Elevation of Entrance Front.
,, 87. "The Wick," Richmond, Surrey: Details of Entrance Front.
,, 88. Ensleigh Lodge, Ham Common, Surrey: Elevation of Entrance Front.
,, 89. Thorncroft Manor, Leatherhead, Surrey: Elevation of Entrance Front.
,, 90. "Hollydale," Keston, Kent: Front Elevation.
,, 91. "Hollydale," Keston, Kent: Details.
,, 92. Pitzhanger Manor, Ealing, London, W.: Front Elevation.
,, 93. Pitzhanger Manor, Ealing, London, W.: External Details and Key Plan.
,, 94. Pitzhanger Manor, Ealing, London, W.: Reading Room, Section and Details.
,, 95. Pitzhanger Manor, Ealing, London, W.: Staircase and Details.
,, 96. Pitzhanger Manor, Ealing, London, W.: Section through Office and Detail of Ceiling.
,, 97. A Vase in the Grounds of Pitzhanger Manor, Ealing, London.
,, 98. Porch from the Manor House, Ham, Surrey: Elevation and Details.
,, 99. Porch, Langham House, Ham, Surrey: Plan, Section, Elevation, Details.
,, 100. Toll Houses, Henley: Elevations and Details.

A VASE, PITZHANGER MANOR, EALING.

Frontispiece

ENTRANCE HALL, No. 1 BEDFORD SQUARE.

INTRODUCTION

EVEN those critics who do not love the work of the late Georgian period, and look askance at its "dull, uninteresting façades," will, in their less guarded moments, grudgingly admit that much of the interior decoration of the period has great charm and beauty. The houses of London in particular have been described as "Palaces hidden behind prison walls," and while by no means admitting the truth of this description, we may concede that there is just sufficient appearance of reason in it to make us pause and consider.

We can quite understand that the visitor from the South of France or Italy, accustomed to the expression of his outdoor life in the elevations of his buildings, might be a little chilled by his first view of, say, Bedford Square (one of the most beautiful, as it is one of the most unspoilt, of the London squares), and if he be chilled with the square, he will be positively frozen by Gower Street! But let us take the same visitor into one of these same "dull" houses. For our purpose we cannot do better than start with the first in the square, and if he be the person of taste and refinement we have taken him for, he will quickly respond to the delicate and restrained detail of the fascinating rooms and chambers.

So it is with most of the late eighteenth-century houses; if we admire the chaste severity of their exteriors, we are charmed and entranced by the innate delicacy of their interiors. Particularly is this true of the smaller houses. We may gaze with wonder upon the elegant splendour of a great Adam saloon at Syon House or Moor Park, and we hasten to add our quota of praise to the skill of the architect, but when our visit to the great house is over, we return to our own modest Georgian house, or visit that of a friend, we

Introduction

are refreshed by the simplicity of the less pretentious dwelling. The small square hall with its gracious staircase, the six-panelled doors with their delicately reeded architraves and neat brass rim locks, the exquisitely proportioned plaster cornices—all have a welcoming and homely air, and as we gratefully rest in front of the old hob grate and admire the proportions and detail of the "Adam" mantelpiece, we feel we understand why he who builds a Versailles must perforce erect a Trianon!

A distinguished American architect once described these smaller Georgian houses as "Models of simplicity with distinction," and they are exactly that; it is this peculiar characteristic of "simplicity with distinction" which differentiates them from all preceding or succeeding works and makes them unique in the history of our domestic architecture.

We have seen how the Palladian tradition persisted until the close of the eighteenth century (see introduction to Vol. 1), how this tradition was modified, if not revolutionized by Robert Adam and his followers, and how the "Colonial" work of America reacted on the architecture of the Mother Country. Adam's clients for the most part were great personages in the fashionable world of his day, and to some extent the capriciousness of all fashionable society is reflected in his work.

After a time one tires of those ornate ceilings and endless arabesques; the very brilliance of the artist dazzles and fatigues.

He was essentially the architect of the large country house and town mansion, but probably the most enduring monument to his memory exists in the great school or tradition he founded, for his influence was immediate and far-reaching, both in this country and America.

Critics complain with some justification that we use the name of "Adam" to describe a multiplicity of works with which he could not conceivably have been connected as if he were the actual author, and though in a literal sense the critics are undoubtedly right in their objection, nevertheless the instinct they condemn is a perfectly sound and natural one.

For if Robert Adam were not the actual author of these buildings, it was his influence which inspired and moulded them, giving that special impress which is so characteristic of his time. If any one man can be said to have created a style, then that one man was Robert Adam.

It is only to-day, when we have shed, or are shedding, the scales which grew over our eyes during the long ugly night of the industrial period, that we can appreciate at their full worth these modest and distinguished homes. Now that we are sufficiently removed from

Introduction

the panorama of the Classic tradition on these islands we can survey with selective and critical taste the various achievements of the great Classic builders who from the time of Inigo Jones to the early years of the nineteenth century followed one another in continuous and unbroken succession.

We see the vigorous splendour and spaciousness of Inigo Jones's Italianate buildings giving place to the more native genius of Wren's, and these in their turn are followed by the works of Hawksmoor and of that eccentric builder but great artist Vanbrugh down to the days of Sir Robert Taylor, Chambers, and Robert Adam.

These were the men who built the great public buildings and proud domestic palaces, but ever in their wake followed a nameless company of humble builders whose work was to provide habitations for cottager, yeoman, and small country squire.

And if these smaller people, working out of the limelight and far from the plaudits of the great lords and ladies who patronized the famous artists, did not achieve for themselves any great personal or individual distinction, it is certain that by their united efforts they formed a great tradition of sound and beautiful building, the full significance of which we are only just beginning to appreciate.

According to our various tastes and predilections we admire this or that phase of Classical building (unless we be so apathetic that we admire none of it), the spaciousness of Inigo Jones, the broad homeliness of Wren and the early Georgian builders, or the charm and distinction of the later.

As long as we concern ourselves with superficial differences and details we shall be a-quarrelling, but directly we dive deeper and examine principles so surely shall we find ourselves in a wonderful unanimity of agreement.

It is not a question of whether one admires the later Georgian builders and rejects the earlier—loves Adam and hates Wren—despises Vanbrugh and respects Inigo Jones. Rather it is a question of what did these men stand for—what principles of beauty and construction did their buildings exemplify?

We shall continue to walk the endless treadmill of styles and revivals until we leave the particular for the general, and examine principles and movements rather than personalities and details.

At this hour of the clock to concern ourselves with one style—even if it be the later Georgian!—is to stultify our taste and deaden our appreciation.

Indeed, we cannot properly understand any one style or period until we can appreciate at its true value what preceded it and what came after.

Introduction

The artist is sensitive to all manifestations of beauty, and even if we be absorbed in admiration of some late Georgian building, yet let us not neglect to peep over our shoulder at the earlier rivals of Queen Anne and Tudor times.

This claim for tolerance must not be read as meaning an easy appreciation of anything and everything, but rather a diligent perseverance and unwearying effort to discover the best in all periods. So shall our convictions have the force of a wedge or driving point with the whole weight of artistic achievement throughout the ages behind us.

Such then is the mood in which we should study the works of the period, which is the subject of this book, viewing them with the critical sympathy of the creative artist rather than with the analytical detachment of the purely intellectual critic.

In the selection of the subjects for illustration the aim throughout has been to amplify and explain those shown in the first volume, and where possible interior views of the houses have been chosen for illustration.

As will be seen, many of the elevations of these houses are shown by measured drawings, and detailed photographs of doors, porches, and garden furniture have also been added.

The choice of the subjects for the interior views presented rather greater difficulties, as many of the houses illustrated in the earlier book contained very little, if anything, of outstanding architectural importance, and in some cases really good and interesting interiors had been spoilt by nineteenth-century vandalism.

Whereas, in producing the first volume, it was the intention to illustrate more particularly the small isolated, or detached, house, and as far as possible the country or suburban types, in preference to those of the towns, in this present volume it has been thought advisable to include a rather greater number of town houses, and, in particular, a certain number of London houses.

As far as possible the subjects have been chosen to illustrate the smaller and less ambitious class of house, in contradistinction to the large town house or country mansion, and if in one or two examples details from the larger houses are shown, it is hoped that their inclusion may be justified on the grounds that the simplicity of treatment is such that they might with equal suitability have graced a far smaller type of house.

As was only to have been expected, London as the capital has the finest examples of the interior work of this period.

No. 1 Bedford Square (see Plates 7–12) is a gem of the first water, and an almost perfect example of what a lesser town house

Introduction

should be. As we wander through these small but exquisite apartments we are amazed at the fertility of invention and the perfect poise maintained by the architect throughout. Built by Thomas Leverton in 1771, it is one of the most delightful houses in a very delightful square.

As is well known to all students of architecture, Robert Adam wrought considerable changes in the planning of the houses he built as compared with those of his predecessors. He was almost as great an innovator in his planning as in his decoration.

Not only did he learn much from the Romans as to their use of ornament, but he seems to have equally profited by the study of their plans. He, and his brothers, loved the long suites of apartments axially planned, and seemed to have had an almost wilful preference for a circular or octagonal, rather than a square, room. And it is to his example that we owe the fertility of invention, both in decoration and in plan, of the late eighteenth-century designers. They may in their treatment at times have been a little finicking and over-refined, but they were never dull. There is a freshness and candour about their work which recalls the springtime of the Renaissance in Italy, when Brunelleschi burst upon the world with his vision of a new and enchanting beauty.

The last of the English Renaissance builders had something of the spontaneity of the earlier Italians, and before they gave place to the pedantic dullness of the Greek Revivalists or the stodgy heaviness of the Victorian Italianists they evolved a series of buildings which within the limits of their problem cannot be surpassed.

Robert Adam's contemporaries may be divided into two, if not three, Schools. There were those who, like Henry Holland (for an example of whose work see Plate 36), Thomas Leverton and Robert Milne, worked in the Adam manner, and in the opposite camp were the guardians of the Palladian tradition, of whom the chiefs were Sir William Chambers, Sir Robert Taylor, and Carr, of York. Each of these renowned leaders had his own little array of retainers and camp followers, who spread the tradition and fame of their chief.

In the third group may be placed the irregulars—Batty-Langley and the "Gothicists," with Stuart and Revett the heralds of the Greek revival.

The names of the leaders connote the characteristic work of the period, for they may be taken as the heads of the various predominant schools.

Of the Palladian group, Sir William Chambers was the most distinguished architect of his generation. He was in every way the opposite of Robert Adam. Whereas Adam was for the most part

Introduction

concerned with domestic architecture in erecting houses for the "nobility and gentry," Chambers did very little in the way of house-building, but was, on the contrary, much concerned with public and semi-public work.

It is said that Chambers hated Adam and all his works—the conservative traditionalist against the aristocratic revolutionary—it is certain that Chambers succeeded in keeping Adam out of the Royal Academy, and it was probably owing to Sir William's opposition that Robert Adam escaped the doubtful distinction of a title!

The study of these two men, both in their contrasting characters and in their work, is extremely interesting.

They both published books for the edification and instruction of the public and their brother architects, and here again we see the difference between the two men in their choice of subjects.

Chambers's work, "A Treatise on Civil Architecture," laid down the rules and regulations to be observed by the Classic builders who followed humbly in the steps of Palladio, Inigo Jones, and Sir William Chambers; whilst Adam, with due Scottish modesty, published a complete edition of his own works and designs!

Chambers's great life-work was the building of Somerset House. He has been called a cold and frigid architect by many critics who compare his gracious reserve with the more characteristically English spontaneity of Wren, with his large free gestures, disdain of detail, and truly British compromise on principles.

Wren is, and will always be, the great national architect, and if in the light of his lantern Chambers's own little candle burns somewhat less brightly, nevertheless, Chambers was a very accomplished architect, and his work was a very necessary and useful corrective to the ornamental exuberance of that of the brothers Adam.

As was only to be expected, the work of both schools reacted on one another, and it is probably owing to this "meeting of the waters" that the work which immediately followed that of Chambers and Adam, chiefly in regard to the smaller houses, and particularly in America, was so simply satisfying and original.

If either of these rival schools had greatly predominated, the result would have been vastly different. With too much Chambers we should have had another period of domestic dullness comparable to that which immediately followed Wren, or, to come nearer to our own time, comparable to the effect of the "Classic" houses which immediately followed the early Victorian.

On the other hand, if Robert Adam had held undisputed sway, the chances are that the latter work of the eighteenth century would have frittered itself away in mere ornamentation and prettiness.

Introduction

Chambers, as we know, did very little purely domestic work, and was probably much too busy on his public buildings to concern himself with small houses—the room illustrated on Plates 16 and 17, from a house in Berners Street, though there is no direct evidence (as far as I know) that it was designed by him, is in his manner.

We know that about the time this house was built (1767) Chambers was living in this locality, and it is quite probable that he actually designed this soberly attractive apartment.

A rather interesting example of the fusion of the "Palladian" and "Adam" traditions is seen in the decoration of the drawing-room from Kent House, Hammersmith Mall (Plate 33), where the ceiling and details generally bear evidence of Adam influence, whilst the fireplace is conceived more in the manner of Chambers.

Amongst the "Palladianists" who carried out a great deal of domestic work is Sir Robert Taylor. See Asgill House, Richmond (Plates 26–30 in this volume and Plate 31, vol. I), and Thorncroft Manor, Leatherhead (Plate 33, vol. I).

Taylor was a conscientious architect, whose best work is not without a certain distinction, and at times even of originality—as, for example, the fireplace from Asgill House, illustrated on Plate 30. But, generally speaking, his work is a little tight and cramped—it has neither the robust conviction of Chambers nor the delicate charm of Adam. He was a useful "general of division," who could always be depended upon for a perfectly sound and creditable performance without in any way displaying great gifts of leadership or originality of thought.

To conclude with our gallery of famous eighteenth-century architects, we next come to a very different type of artist in Sir John Soane.

Soane is one of those architects, examples of which occur in all countries at different times, who have probably suffered as much from the extravagant praises of their admirers as from the depreciation of hostile critics.

At one time it was the fashion to regard him as the exponent of all that was false and theatrical in architecture. The pendulum has now swung to the other extreme, and his reputation is in danger of being permanently damaged by a wave of unreasoning enthusiasm.

To parody a cynicism attributed to Disraeli, it might be said of Soane's work that it contained much that was true and much that was original, but unfortunately that which was true was not original and that which was original was not true.

By the end of the eighteenth century the great Classic tradition had become a little thin and attenuated. Disturbing elements were

Introduction

at work, and one sometimes feels that Soane was a sort of architectural Canute, vainly striving to keep back the waves of the disintegrating forces.

There is one aspect of Sir John Soane that will appeal greatly to all modern architects, and that is when one views him as a collector. Soane was a mighty collector both of the works of his contemporaries and of the works of the artists of the past. To-day everyone seems to be a collector—the shop of the antique dealer is to be found in almost every town of any size throughout the country; but we very seldom collect contemporary work. Disgusted with the fatuities of the nineteenth century we are, as it were, seeking frantically to establish a better standard of taste, to gather round us such a collection of beautiful objects that the next generation will possibly accept them as a matter of course, and will then, with eyes trained by the work of the older artists, give rein to the joy of creative effort.

Of Soane's domestic work, the house which he built for himself in Lincoln's Inn Fields (now the Soane Museum) is probably the best known, both to architects and the general public.

It is an interesting mixture of archæology and originality. As we walk through those intercommunicating chambers with their queer umbrella-shaped ceilings, we cannot but admire the ingenuity of the author; for a museum to house an intimate personal collection it is ideal; but as a home it lacks many home-like features.

Pitzhanger Manor at Ealing, now the Ealing Public Library, though not so well known as the Lincoln's Inn building, is in many respects a much finer house and certainly a more comfortable one to live in.

The original house was built by George Dance, junior, in whose office Soane worked, but whilst Soane retained the south wing containing the drawing-room and dining-room which he very much admired (see Plates 42–44 and 92–97), he pulled down the rest of Dance's house and rebuilt the manor on the lines we see there to-day.

Soane's work, like so much of Adam's, suffers from over-elaboration—the amount of interest and detail put into the design of Soane's town residence could with advantage be spread over a dozen houses, instead of being confined to one.

And though this was an error of judgment as far as the simpler type of domestic work was concerned, we can learn much from the study of individual doors, mantelpieces, etc. In fact, both Adam and Soane have this in common, that their work is a perfect mine of inspiration for their followers, who, selecting with greater judgment, or kept in severe check by lack of funds, did in many instances produce work of a sounder artistic worth than that of their masters.

Introduction

From the very earliest days of the Renaissance, the English builders have paid great attention to the entrance hall. Both Inigo Jones and Wren spent infinite pains to attain a fine entrance, and both architects seem to have had a preference for halls running through two stories with a gallery round. One of the finest examples of a hall of this kind is to be seen at the Queen's House, Greenwich, built by Inigo Jones for Henrietta Maria, the wife of Charles I.

In this house, and in many of the houses built in the succeeding centuries, the staircase is found in another apartment adjacent, but in close proximity, to the entrance hall.

In the smaller houses of the late Georgian period—possibly for reasons of economy—the staircase is usually found leading from the entrance hall and forming its most important feature (see Plate 1, Mottram Hall, Cheshire).

These apartments are frequently square or oblong on plan, in some of the more important houses circular or oval, and it is not until we are well into the nineteenth century that we find the roomy entrance hall has been almost entirely superseded by the dark and stuffy passage entrance which seems to have such a peculiar attraction for lodging-house keepers. As is only to be expected, the use of the Classic order in various shapes and sizes is to be found in one place or another throughout these late eighteenth-century houses.

In the entrance halls we frequently find the "Order" used in connexion with a simple arcade, such as that at Greycourt, Ham, or as a pilaster forming part of a wall arcade, as in the entrance hall at Kent House, Hammersmith Mall (see Plate 4).

The early Georgian builders seem to have had a great liking for the Roman Ionic order, with the volutes of the capitals set diagonally, but Robert Adam and the later designers fought rather shy of this type, and, when they used this order, confined themselves to a more Grecian variety of the Ionic. For the most part they appear to have preferred either some variant of the Corinthian for their more elaborate work or the Doric in all its phases. In fact, for the simple work and the smaller houses, there is no doubt that the Doric order is first favourite. This is probably due as much to motives of economy as to suitability of shape and design. It is, of course, the simplest of all the orders, and so appropriately goes with simple work.

The floors of these entrance halls were frequently made of large squares of black and white marble or stone laid either square or diagonally, though examples are to be found, particularly in the later houses built at the end of the century, of more elaborate patterns including Greek keys and wave ornaments.

Introduction

In some of Adam's larger houses are to be seen wonderful examples of this artist's treatment as exemplified in the hall with its richly coffered ceiling, elaborate arcading, and decorated niches filled with vases or sculpture.

A good example of Soane's treatment of an entrance hall is to be seen at Pitzhanger Manor, Ealing (Plate 3), which, like most of Soane's work at this house, is simpler in design and conception than his other houses, and for that reason more domestic.

A very fine example of a comparatively small entrance hall treated with consummate skill is that at No. 1 Bedford Square, by Thomas Leverton, which forms the subject of the frontispiece. Here we have an example of shallow arches and flat saucer-like dome which seems to suggest an intelligent anticipation of one of Soane's favourite combinations, but how different in spirit from Soane's work!

Everything about Leverton's design is quiet and distinguished. We feel none of that straining after effect, that wilful eccentricity, which is so disturbing a factor in the designs of his successor. Possibly Soane's work is more archæologically correct, but how far removed from the domestic repose of Leverton's?

Many of these late eighteenth-century entrance halls have their walls treated with "marbling," a process which, together with that of "graining," was greatly abused in the succeeding century, and so fell into disrepute.

An interesting example of this "marbling" treatment is to be seen in the entrance hall at Kent House, Hammersmith Mall, already referred to.

Other examples of marbling treatment with scagliola columns, etc., are to be found in the halls of certain houses in Bedford Square. In some cases marble wall-paper of a particularly delightful shade of yellow and brown was used—very different from the horrible marbled papers which are now usually only seen in kitchens and bathrooms. It is rather interesting to note that of late years efforts have been made in Paris to reproduce these marbled papers in their original eighteenth-century colours.

Another interesting example of an entrance hall and staircase treatment is to be seen in a house in Pall Mall designed by Sir John Soane (see Plate 53). Probably Soane is seen here at his best. The design is an honest, straightforward piece of work without any of the freakishness and whimsicalities to be seen both at Pitzhanger and at his house in Lincoln's Inn Fields.

The next feature to be considered in the internal design of these houses is the main staircase, which, as I have said, frequently forms an integral part of the design for the entrance hall.

Introduction

The open-newel staircase, since Elizabethan and Jacobean days, has always been one of the chief glories of English houses.

In Sir Christopher Wren's time the design of the staircase underwent very radical changes, and the Classic staircase as used throughout the eighteenth century is really a refinement and adaptation of his motives.

Wren very frequently used a stone staircase with wrought-iron balusters or balustrade, finished with mahogany handrail, though it is probably not correct to say that he was the first architect to use the stone staircase, as previously Inigo Jones had used this form of stair at the Queen's House, Greenwich.

The use of stone profoundly influenced the design of wooden stairs, and it became the custom to introduce the cut string in imitation of the stone forms. There is a very interesting example of a wooden stair in the early part of Greenwich Hospital, in which the treads are square in shape instead of the spandrel form of later days. This staircase clearly shows traces of a stone prototype.

Both in Inigo Jones's and Wren's days it was the custom for the handrail to run in straight flights, and to stop between heavy newels, but afterwards, in the early Georgian times, this handrail, supported by either twisted or moulded balusters, followed the line of the staircase by a series of ramps. Gradually, as time went on, the handrail became finer in design, and the thick balusters of the earlier architects gave place in the wooden staircases to the finely turned mahogany balusters of the later men, whilst the handrail frequently followed one continuous sweep. Particularly in the town houses, the use of the stone staircase with the iron balustrade is very usual. An interesting example of this is seen in a house by Isaac Ware at the corner of Bloomsbury Square.

Probably the most graceful and refined of these wrought-iron staircases are to be found in the houses which were built from about 1750 to 1780. There is a very fine example of such a staircase designed by Sir Robert Taylor for No. 35 Lincoln's Inn Fields, now to be seen at the Victoria and Albert Museum.

Afterwards the balustrading became much more simple in outline, such as seen in Soane's staircase in the house in Pall Mall already referred to.

The Greek Revivalists who followed Soane very frequently used a delicate cast-iron baluster decorated with acanthus or honeysuckle ornament.

As throughout all the details of the Classic period, the "Order" is used in various forms in these staircases. Sometimes there is a

Introduction

Doric column forming a newel at the end of the staircase, and in other examples a thin Doric column on top of a vase is used for a baluster, particularly in the earlier examples.

An interesting type of wooden staircase is to be seen in Walpole House, Chiswick Mall (see Plate 2). It is rather earlier in date than most of the houses we have under consideration, but forms an interesting link between Queen Anne and the later Georgian examples. Following this we get such a staircase as is to be seen at "Oare" in Wiltshire (see Plate 5), which, although later in date, has much in common with the Walpole House staircase.

The use of the thin iron square baluster in connexion with the stone stairs found its echo in the wooden staircase by the use of a similar baluster in wood. This form came into very general use for the smaller and less expensive houses somewhere about 1780, and, possibly owing to its very cheapness, it became almost universal for the small house in Regency and earlier Victorian days.

If used discriminately with interesting newels and a well-designed handrail, this form of baluster can be made to look very effective; but, as was frequently the case in the early nineteenth century, when it was employed without much thought and mainly on the ground of saving expense, the appearance of the staircase became thin and attenuated, and lost much of the charm of the earlier examples.

In the earlier Georgian staircase where the cut string is employed the spandrel end is frequently finished with very elaborate carved brackets, which, at the end of the century, gave place to a simpler type of bracket such as that of the staircase at Kent House, Hammersmith Mall (Plate 4), where the ornament is in very low relief, or alternatively, as is found in a good many examples, the ornament is entirely omitted.

This staircase also shows the way the handrail was wreathed round at the bottom and supported on a series of small balusters with central newel in the shape of a slim Doric column.

An important feature in connexion with the entrance hall is the treatment of the front door, which may, or may not, have a very important influence on the design of the hall itself.

Rober Adam and his followers were very successful in the use of a beautiful type of lead-glazed fanlight, which was not infrequently carried down on either side of the door in panels. An example of this may be seen on Plate 3, which is the entrance door to No. 35 Bedford Square, and also on Plate 35 of Volume No. 1.

Next in importance to the entrance hall and staircase come the fireplaces of the principal living-rooms.

Introduction

The fireplace in Tudor and late Gothic times was generally nothing more than a decorated hole in the wall finished with a simple stone surround, sometimes in the form of a four-centred arch against which the oak panelling of the room was framed. In Jacobean and Elizabethan times the fireplace with the wall over became a much more glorious affair, frequently framed in free standing "Orders" of elaborate design. The panelling over was treated with intricate strap-work ornament; but the actual fireplace opening itself was still a hole in the wall for burning wood logs on iron dogs.

In Carolean and Queen Anne days the fireplace reverted to a simpler and more natural treatment.

Wren was frequently content with either a wood or marble bolection moulding round his fireplace opening with wood panelling framed against it, somewhat on Tudor lines, but of a very different design, and not infrequently carving of the Grinling Gibbon's type was introduced in the wall panelling over the fireplace.

As the fireplace developed in Georgian days the "Order" was frequently used in some form or other in connexion with the design of the fireplace surround.

Interesting examples of the late Palladian treatment of fireplaces are to be seen in Plate 33, at Kent House, Hammersmith Mall, and at 21 Berners Street (Plate 16). It is interesting to compare these fireplaces with those designed by Robert Adam and his followers. Such as, for example, the fireplaces from a house in Hatton Garden and at Kelmscott House, Hammersmith (Plates 39–40), where the use of the thin delicate "Order" with beautifully enriched mouldings and exquisite low relief ornament afford examples of the Classic English fireplace in the full glory of the culminating period.

These late eighteenth-century fireplaces are amongst the most typical features of the houses of that date. Probably Robert Adam himself spent more time and took more trouble over the design of his fireplaces than over any other features in his houses. In addition to the carved wood mantelpiece decorated with low relief, such as, for example, that from a house in Edinburgh (shown on Plate 41), Adam loved to use all kinds of marble with carved panels, brackets, and orders enriched by the use of simple bands of inlaid marble of a different colour.

Some twenty or thirty years ago these late eighteenth-century fireplaces could be acquired for a mere song, but, fortunately, their artistic value is very much better appreciated to-day, and it is not unusual to find in the lease of the London houses descriptions of these fireplaces and a clause forbidding the tenant to alter or remove them,

Introduction

and any substitution is guarded against by the attachment of photographs of the fireplace referred to.

The use of marble during the later part of the eighteenth century for the fireplace surround is to be found even in the very smallest houses. Of course, the design was correspondingly more simple. The use of flat-reeded architraves with simple rosettes at the corners and plain reeded shelf over is the most usual form.

A very attractive and inexpensive mantelpiece extensively used throughout this period is the wooden fireplace surround enriched with composition ornament, and innumerable examples are to be found in this country and in the colonial work of America which testify to the fertile imagination of their designers. Small panels containing groups of cupids or other Classic mythological figures are frequently to be seen in the centre of the frieze, or over the ends of pilasters, surrounded with mouldings decorated in low relief. Vases, wreaths, swags, together with conventional treatment of bunches of grapes and wheatsheaves are alternative subjects for decoration.

The shelf itself, as with the more simple marble ones, is not infrequently finished with a reeded edge, but in the more elaborate examples this shelf is moulded and has a bed-mould, sometimes composed of several members enriched by dentils, leaf and tongue ornament, etc., or in some cases with an elaborate form of pear-drop ornament. As an example of this wood and composition treatment, see measured drawing of fireplace from a house in the Paragon at Blackheath, Plate 66.

The fireplace opening itself was very generally finished with simple slabs of marble some 6 in. wide at the sides and top immediately adjacent to the wooden surround.

In the earlier examples the open fire with iron dogs is still found, but Robert Adam and his school were responsible for the introduction of the very beautiful types of basket and hob-grates which were used so extensively throughout the last half of the eighteenth century.

These grates are triumphs of the metal-workers' art, and for beauty of finish and delicacy of design can only be compared to certain Louis XVI and "Empire" grates to be found in France.

About this time, too, fenders came into general use, a very typical form being that of pierced steel or brass, sometimes the two metals being used in combination.

In Regency and earlier Victorian days the use of brass mountings and enrichments were also employed for the decoration of the grate itself.

Introduction

There was, during the latter half of the eighteenth century and the earlier years of the nineteenth, a slight but marked influence due to French design. We realize this particularly when we study certain articles of furniture designed by Robert Adam, and we see it again in connexion with fireplaces of the Regency and earlier Victorian days. An example of this influence may be seen in the fireplace of Lincoln's Inn Fields (see Plate 35).

No detail of the house was considered too mean for the attention of these late eighteenth-century architects and designers—fenders, bell-pulls, door furniture, all received consideration at their hands. One feature in which they particularly gloried was the treatment of mirrors. Many fine examples of designs for mirrors are to be found in Robert Adam's book on his own work.

The late Georgian builders do not appear to have been so fond of wood panelling for the finishing of their rooms as the earlier Georgian. Plaster-work during this period made great advances. These late eighteenth-century houses contain a wealth of delicate and refined plaster-work.

One very favourite *motif* is to be found in the introduction of classic figures in panels on the wall over the fireplace, set off with swags or foliated ornament in low relief (see Plates 55–56). The upper part of the walls themselves were not infrequently treated with broad, simple panelling formed with plaster mouldings, the mouldings themselves being small in scale and sometimes enriched. The lower part of the wall was finished as a plain dado with a moulded chair rail. This chair rail frequently taking the form of a running dentil course, or delicately moulded leaf and tongue work finished with a plain fascia and small cyma.

The treatment of the walls was very carefully considered in relation to the design of the ceiling, which came next in importance to the design of the fireplace, the centre of interest in the room.

The earlier plaster ceilings of Inigo Jones and Wren were much heavier in design, with endless bands of foliage and with strongly marked cofferings and mouldings. The earlier Georgian architects continued with variations of these themes, but the later men were much more revolutionary. Here there was no suggestion of plaster imitating stone forms. The lowest of low relief was used, and the most conventional of patterns.

In the design of the best ceilings of this period, as with all the other details of the late eighteenth-century house, the influence of Robert Adam is all-powerful.

If we compare a genuine Adam ceiling—such as the ceiling of St. James's club-house, formerly Coventry House, Piccadilly (see

Introduction

Plate 49), or the ceiling of No. 3 Adelphi Terrace (see Plate 48)—with those at Nos. 1 and 2 Bedford Square, this influence will easily be understood.

Many of the more important ceilings had small panels painted by Angelica Kauffmann and her disciples, and even to-day, some 140 years after they were painted, these panels, though somewhat mellowed by the hand of time, are still extraordinarily vivid in colour and tone.

It is a useful experience actually to measure some of the mouldings and plaster-work of these ceilings, and it will come as a surprise to many to find how small the various members are.

The juncture of the ceiling with the wall received the most careful consideration. In some cases, as in the drawing-room to No. 1 Bedford Square (see Plate 12), the ceiling treatment is continued on to the wall itself with a small frieze decorated with low relief ornament of a conventional kind. Personally, I do not feel that this example is altogether satisfactory, and in my opinion the design of the room would have been better if this particular frieze had been omitted.

Other examples of frieze treatments, but with rather happier effect, are to be seen on Plate 50, from another house in the square.

Two very interesting examples of ceilings are to be seen in a house in Dublin (see Plate 45), which are very different in inception from those we have been looking at. Here there is a strong French influence dating from the rococo work of Louis XV. Another ceiling which shows traces of French influence is to be seen in the view of the room at No. 21 Berners Street (see Plate 16).

There is often a good deal of confusion of thought between the essential characteristics of Louis XIV and Louis XV work. Louis XIV decoration was, like Louis XIV himself, imposing and dominating in character, more suited to the magnificent salon of a great palace than the intimate apartment of a private house, but the best of the Louis XV work which followed—although much more capricious than that of the preceding period—has a delicacy and charm which peculiarly confines it to the decoration of small and intimate apartments.

Probably the greatest contrast between an early Georgian and late Georgian house, and one which will immediately strike the attention of the most casual beholder, is the difference in the colour schemes employed.

The principle rooms of a Queen Anne and earlier Georgian house were generally panelled with a dark oak, such as we see in Wren's work at Hampton Court, or in pine wood panelling painted a dark

Introduction

green with the enrichments in some cases picked out in gold; or as an alternative scheme these early Georgian houses had their panelling and walls painted white or cream colour. The later architects preferred colours of a much lower tone, and here again we see the influence of the French. Walls painted café-au-lait, light greys, and dove colours, or light greens and blues predominated.

Ceilings were for the most part kept white or cream, and in the more important examples had their enrichments picked out in gold, with the little painted panels already described worked in as part of the general scheme. Painted panels were not confined to the ceiling, but were occasionally used also for wall decorations, such as the example at the octagonal room, Asgill House (see Plate 28), and in Boodle's Clubhouse (see Plate 37).

In the entrance hall to Asgill House there are some very interesting examples of grisaille painting. Unfortunately, owing to difficulties of lighting, it was impossible to obtain an adequate photograph of this hall. Soane and the early nineteenth-century architects frequently introduced darker colours in the form of tuscan red, terra-cotta, pompeian greens, blue, and yellows into their decoration.

Wall-papers were very largely used in the smaller houses and cottages. The design of these papers generally reflected either Eastern influences, in the form of Chinese design on glazed paper or followed some native chintz pattern of little flowers or trellis work diapered over a light ground.

Another very important feature in these houses was the treatment of the doors and the door surrounds. The six-panelled door of the earlier Georgians continued its popularity, although the mouldings were slightly reduced in size and frequently the raised panel was omitted. Occasionally reedings took the place of mouldings, and in some of the later doors ebony inlay was introduced.

Some of the most beautiful doors in the more important houses are of polished mahogany with panels formed of fluted margins having low relief rosettes at the corners.

Sir William Chambers and the Palladianists frequently used an "Order" with entablature over for the surround of their doors, or a simple architrave with enriched pulvinated frieze and cornice over. See, for example, door to dining-room, Asgill House, Richmond (Plate 27), and doorway to Ely House, Dover Street (Plate 14), both designed by Sir Robert Taylor.

On the other hand, Adam, Leverton, and others seem to have preferred the use of brackets, usually of a slight projection, with low relief ornament in place of such orders to carry pediments or

Introduction

cornices over their doors. Plate 13 shows two very beautiful doors from Kenwood, Middlesex. Although Kenwood cannot be called a "small" house, these two doors are excellent examples of a type of door, more or less ornate, which were used in innumerable small houses throughout the country. These remarks also apply to the door from Harewood House, Hanover Square, now, unfortunately, demolished, which is also another authentic Adam door.

In connexion with the doors some little attention should be given to the very excellent metalwork in the shape of door furniture that was used. In the smaller houses we find simple brass rim locks with plain, round, or drop handles of the same material, whilst in the doors of the larger houses there is to be found chased and gilt door furniture of a very exquisite character.

In the first volume some reference was made to the influence of Batty Langley and the Gothic Romanticists. Their work is less in evidence in interior decoration than in exterior. We find this influence chiefly reflected in the use of those interlacing glazing bars in the fronts of bookcases and cupboards, so much beloved by the late eighteenth-century architect and furniture maker.

Eighteenth-century furniture, if not actually designed by the architects, was largely inspired by them. They were particularly successful in their provision and treatment of cupboards. Cupboards should be designed in connexion with the planning and decoration of the room, and with some regard to the particular places they have to fill. They are not infrequently amongst the most pleasing and memorable of the features of an old house.

As an example of a particularly fine built-in piece of furniture see Plate 51, which shows a bookcase in the form of a series of shelves designed by Robert Adam. The last half of the eighteenth century was also the culminating period in English furniture.

The walnut furniture of William and Mary and Queen Anne had given place to the mahogany of Chippendale, which in its turn was followed by the elegant pieces of Sheraton and Hepplewhite, afterwards to be superseded by the less interesting work of Vulliamy and the men of the Regency, who, accepting the tradition of the architecture of their time, showed less of natural craftsmanship and more of research in their work.

To again mention Robert Adam—from whom one cannot escape when dealing with this period—one has only to turn to his book of designs to see what a great interest he took in furniture and accessories. Amongst other innovations he introduced a particularly fascinating form of painted furniture. In this respect he was followed by Hepplewhite and a great many other craftsmen of the

Introduction

period who produced very many useful and simple pieces, such as chairs, sofas, card-tables, etc., of painted or lacquered wood enriched with floral or figured decoration painted in contrasting colours.

Some of the most striking of this furniture was made of rose and satinwood veneers on a framework of white wood or mahogany. Towards the end of the century veneers of all descriptions, including finely figured mahoganies, were used extensively.

In connexion with the furnishing of these rooms some mention must be made of curtains and window treatments, which received very careful attention at the hands of both architect and decorator.

In the simpler houses plain valance boards with curtains and valances of either chintz or silk damask were used, but in the more elaborate wonderfully designed window-heads of carved and gilt wood or plaster-work were used to cover the valance boards and form a finish to the curtains.

Gradually the glories of the eighteenth century house craftsmanship gave place to the trivialities of the early Victorian, and finally flickered out in the vagaries of the Italian revival.

The Industrial Age was upon us, and it was to be many long years before we were again to see anything worthy to rank with the English house of the later Georgian period.

During the last thirty years or so there has been a revival of better methods in the building and designing of our domestic dwellings, both in this country and America.

Our own Georgian revival has reacted upon the revival of colonial work in the States, and the American colonial work is to-day in its turn making its influence felt on our own practice. It is evident to the most casual observer that in late years, both here and on the other side of the Atlantic, a renewed and vigorous interest is being taken in the houses and furniture of the late eighteenth century, an interest which, it is hoped, the work shown in this book may do something to stimulate and develop still further.

STANLEY C. RAMSEY.

ENTRANCE HALL, MOTTRAM HALL, CHESHIRE.

STAIRCASE, WALPOLE HOUSE, CHISWICK MALL.

Plate 3

ENTRANCE PITZHANGER MANOR, EALING.

ENTRANCE, No. 35 BEDFORD SQUARE.

Plate 4

ENTRANCE HALL, KENT HOUSE, THE MALL, HAMMERSMITH.

ENTRANCE HALL, GRAY COURT, HAM.

Plate 5

STAIRCASE, "OARE," PEWSEY, WILTS.

Plate 6

"OARE," PEWSEY, WILTS.

Plate 7

ENTRANCE HALL, No. 1 BEDFORD SQUARE.

Plate 8

THE STAIRCASE, No. 1 BEDFORD SQUARE.

DINING-ROOM, No. 1 BEDFORD SQUARE.

DINING-ROOM, No. 1 BEDFORD SQUARE.

Plate 11

A CHIMNEYPIECE IN No. 1 BEDFORD SQUARE.

Plate 12

DRAWING-ROOM, No. 1 BEDFORD SQUARE.

DRAWING-ROOM, No. 1 BEDFORD SQUARE.

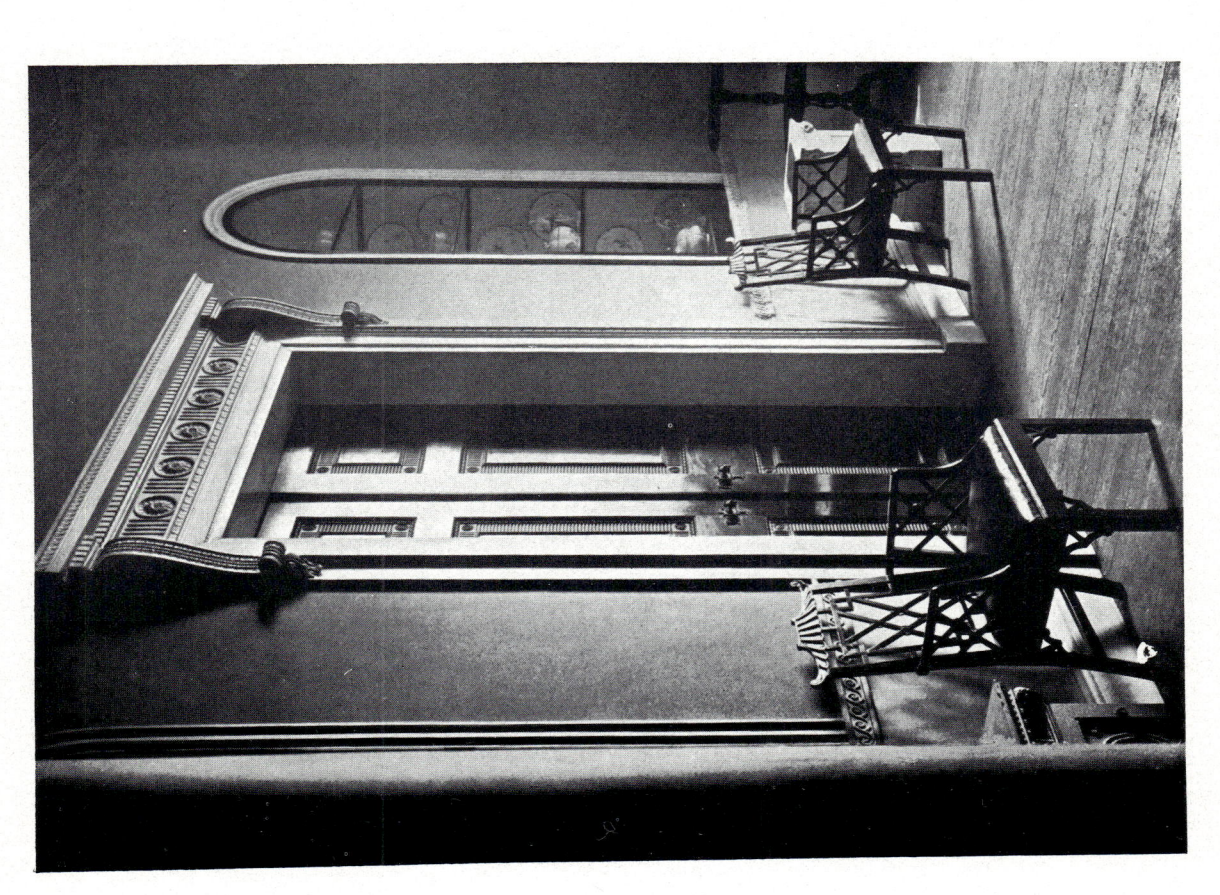

TWO DOORWAYS AT KENWOOD, HAMPSTEAD.

Plate 14

DINING-ROOM DOORWAY, ELY HOUSE, DOVER STREET, LONDON.
SIR ROBERT TAYLOR, ARCHITECT.

Plate 15

STAIRCASE HALL, ELY HOUSE, DOVER STREET, LONDON, W.

Plate 16

21 BERNERS STREET, W.

DOORWAY IN 21 BERNERS STREET, LONDON.

DOORWAY AT HAREWOOD HOUSE, HANOVER SQUARE, LONDON.
(Now Demolished.)

STAIRCASE, EAST CLIFF HOUSE, HASTINGS.

No. 2 BEDFORD SQUARE.

DRAWING-ROOM, 13 BEDFORD SQUARE.

Plate 22

CARVED WOOD CHIMNEYPIECE (NOW IN THE VICTORIA AND ALBERT MUSEUM).

Plate 23

CHIMNEY-PIECE FROM AN OLD HOUSE IN CANONBURY PLACE, LONDON.

Plate 24

END BAY OF DRAWING-ROOM, STONE HOUSE, LEWISHAM.

Plate 25

DRAWING-ROOM, STONE HOUSE, LEWISHAM.

Plate 26

ASGILL HOUSE, RICHMOND.

Plate 27

A DOORWAY, ASGILL HOUSE, RICHMOND.

ASGILL HOUSE, RICHMOND.

Plate 29

BEDROOM IN ASGILL HOUSE, RICHMOND.

Plate 30

FIREPLACE AT ASGILL HOUSE, RICHMOND.

Plate 31

MANTELPIECE IN A HOUSE AT SHEEN, NEAR RICHMOND, SURREY.

FIREPLACE IN WALPOLE HOUSE, CHISWICK MALL.

Plate 33

FIREPLACE IN KENT HOUSE, HAMMERSMITH MALL.

Plate 34

London Survey Committee. *Photograph by A. H. Blake.*

ARCHWAY ON FIRST FLOOR, 91 CHEYNE WALK, CHELSEA.

DETAIL OF STAIRCASE, GRAY COURT, HAM.

Plate 35

WINDOW IN THE PREMISES OF GILL & REIGATE, LTD.,
THE SOHO GALLERIES.

L.C.C. Photograph.

FIREPLACE FROM 51 LINCOLN'S INN FIELDS.

THE LARGE SMOKING-ROOM, BROOKS'S CLUB HOUSE, LONDON.

THE SALOON, BOODLE'S CLUB HOUSE, LONDON.

Plate 38

FIREPLACES IN No. 7 GREAT GEORGE STREET, BRISTOL.

Plate 39

London Survey Committee. Photograph by Edward Yates.

KELMSCOTT HOUSE, HAMMERSMITH MALL.
FIREPLACE IN DINING-ROOM.

Plate 40

Photo: E. Dockree.

CHIMNEY-PIECE FROM A HOUSE IN HATTON GARDEN, LONDON.

Plate 41

CARVED PINE FIREPLACE, FORMERLY IN A HOUSE IN EDINBURGH.

Plate 42

PITZHANGER MANOR, EALING.

PITZHANGER MANOR, EALING.

STAIRCASE, PITZHANGER MANOR, EALING.

PITZHANGER MANOR, EALING.

Plate 45

CEILING, BELVEDERE HOUSE, DUBLIN.

ST. STEPHEN'S CLUB, DUBLIN. DETAIL OF CEILING.

Plate 46

CEILING AT KENT HOUSE, HAMMERSMITH.

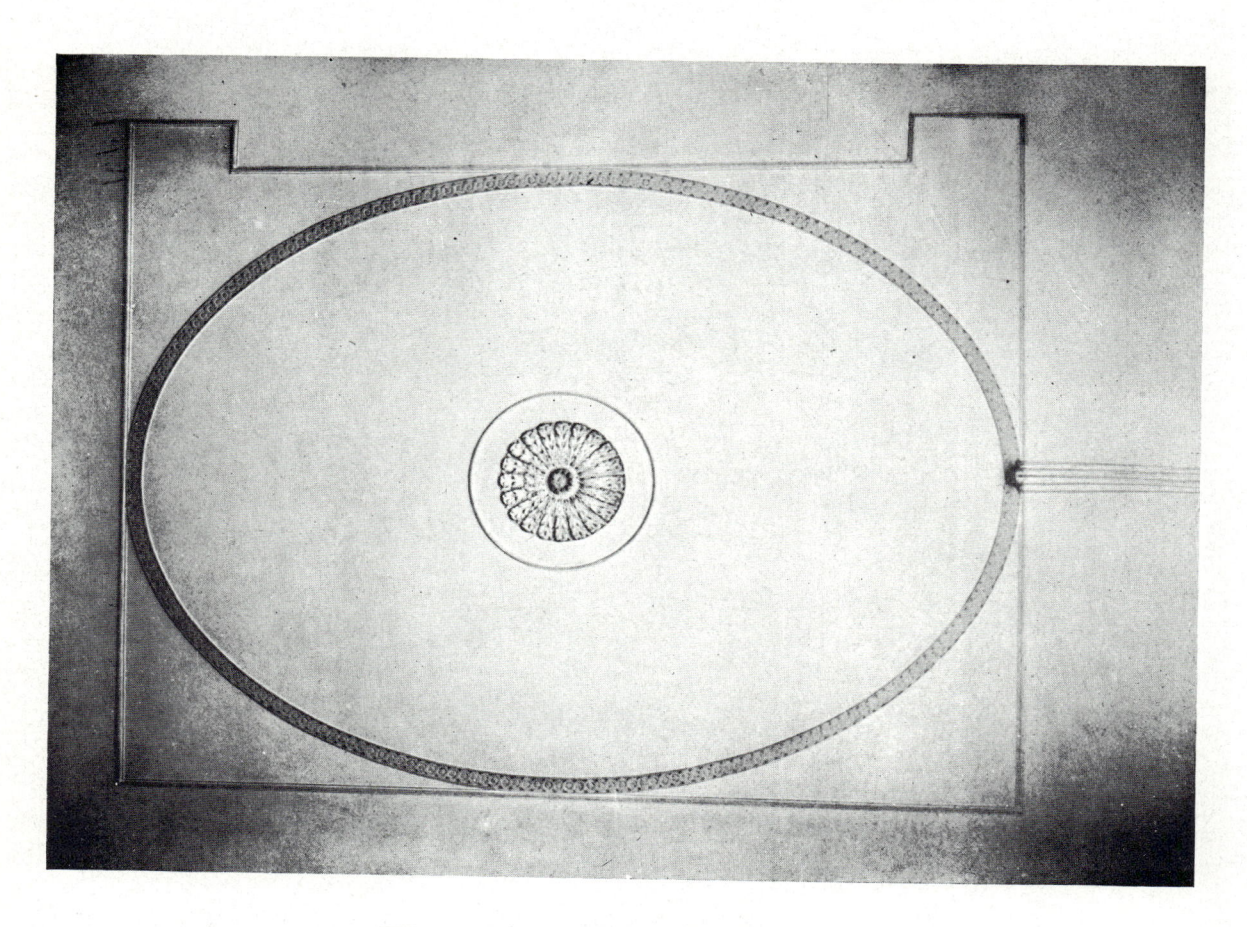

CEILING AT No. 2 BEDFORD SQUARE.

Plate 47

TWO LONDON CHIMNEYPIECES OF MARBLE.

Plate 48

CEILING, 3 ADELPHI TERRACE, LONDON. ROBERT ADAM, ARCHITECT.

CENTRAL BAY OF COFFEE-ROOM CEILING, ST. JAMES'S CLUB, LONDON.

DETAILS OF FRIEZES AT 35 BEDFORD SQUARE.

Plate 51

DETAIL OF A LATE EIGHTEENTH CENTURY BOOKCASE

Plate 52

L.C.C. Photograph.

CEILING FROM No. 65 LINCOLN'S INN FIELDS.

L.C.C. Photograph.

CEILING FROM No. 51 LINCOLN'S INN FIELDS.

THE OVAL STAIRCASE HALL IN THE OLD WAR OFFICE, PALL MALL, LONDON (NOW DEMOLISHED). SIR JOHN SOANE, ARCHITECT.

Plate 54

DOORCASE FROM No. 29 GREAT GEORGE STREET, WESTMINSTER, NOW IN THE VICTORIA AND ALBERT MUSEUM, SOUTH KENSINGTON.

Plate 55

PLASTER OVERMANTEL FROM No. 25 PARLIAMENT STREET, WESTMINSTER, NOW IN THE VICTORIA AND ALBERT MUSEUM.

Plate 56

PLASTER MEDALLION FROM No. 29 GREAT GEORGE STREET, WESTMINSTER.

Plate 57

London Survey Committee. *Photograph by H. W. Fincham.*

CATHERINE LODGE, TRAFALGAR SQUARE, CHELSEA.
VIEW OF STAIRCASE.

Plate 58

DETAIL OF ENTRANCE FRONT. DETAIL OF ENTRANCE ARCH.
PITZHANGER MANOR, EALING.

Plate 59

GARDEN DETAILS AT PITZHANGER HOUSE, EALING.

ENTRANCE TO THE MANOR HOUSE, HAM.

Plate 61

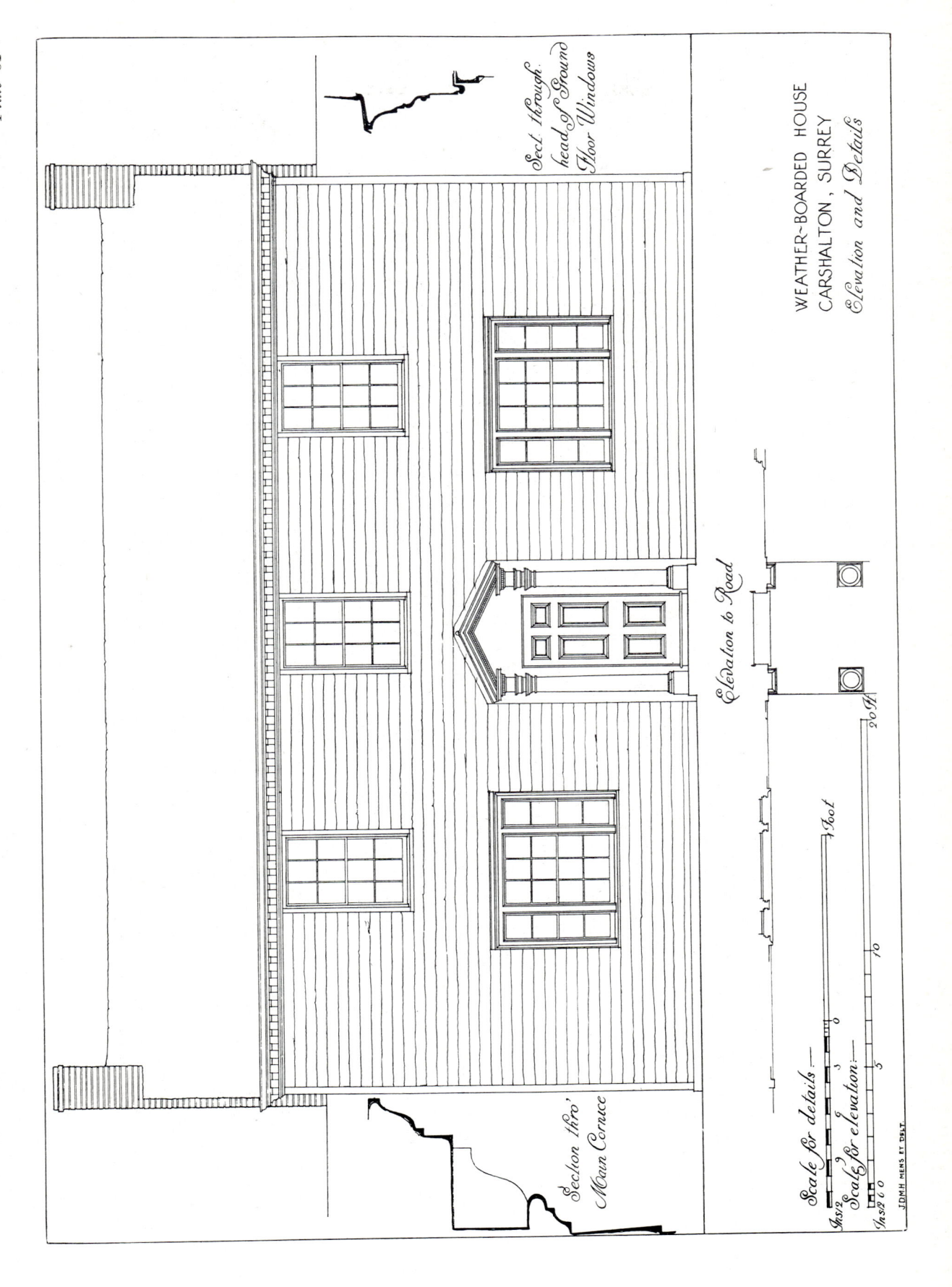

Sect. through head of Ground floor Windows

Section thro' Main Cornice

Elevation to Road

WEATHER-BOARDED HOUSE
CARSHALTON, SURREY
Elevation and Details

Scale for details
Scale for elevation

Plate 62

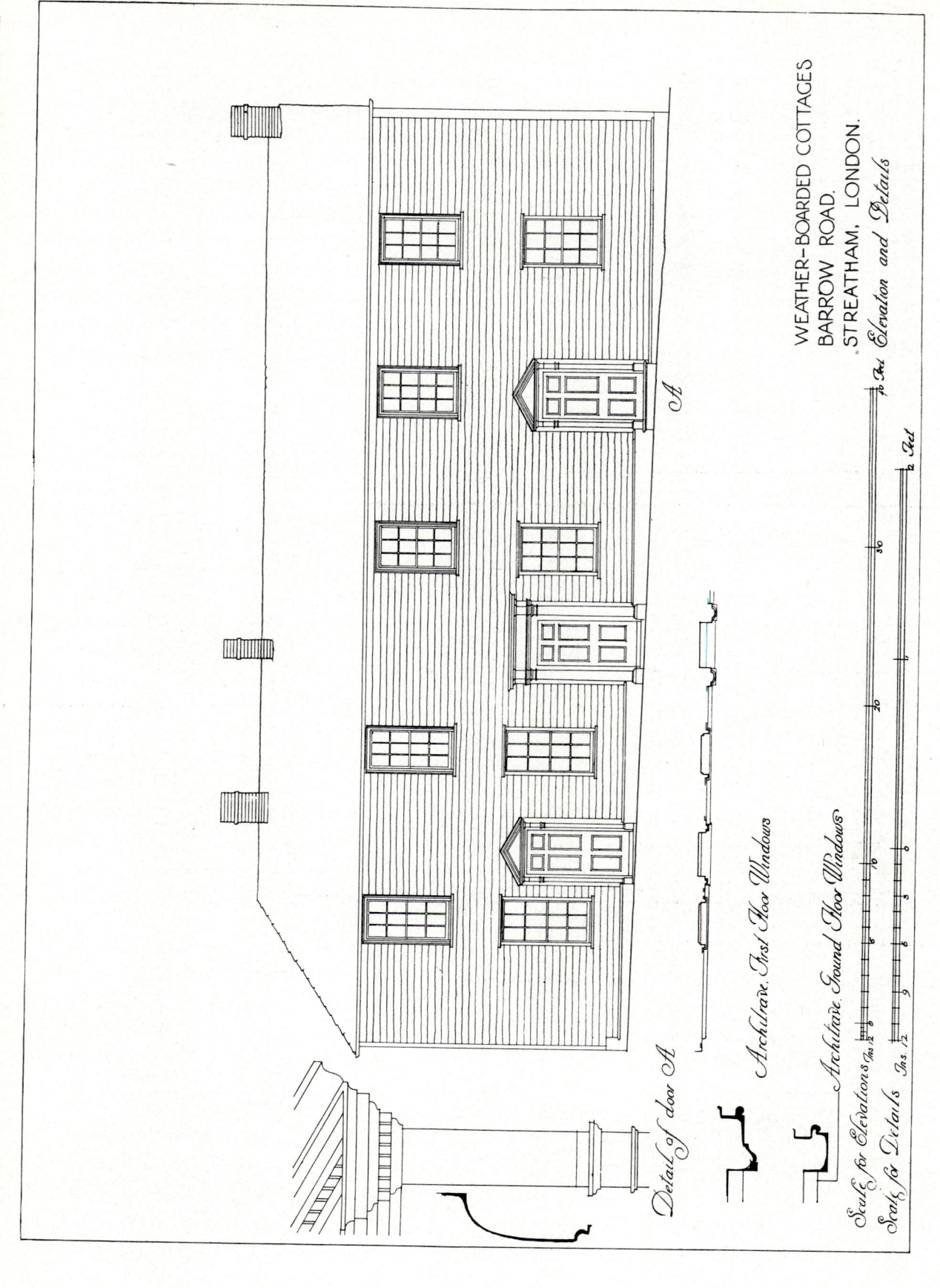

Detail of door A

Architrave. First Floor Windows

Architrave. Ground Floor Windows

WEATHER-BOARDED COTTAGES
BARROW ROAD.
STREATHAM. LONDON.
Elevation and Details

Scale for Elevations Ins.12
Scale for Details Ins.12

Plate 63

Section

Fanlight Removed

Elevation

Detail of Order.

Architrave of Fanlight.

Panel mould.

Impost moulding.

Base of Column.

Quarter-plan at "A"

Quarter-plan at "B"

Scales for:
Elev: Details: Panel
12 Ins. 12 Ins. 12 Ins.

PORCH, ASHLEY HOUSE
EPSOM, SURREY.
Elevation, Section
& Details

Plate 64

Scale for Elevations

Section

Elevation

Scale for Details

Scale for Ironwork

Detail of Entablature

Half-Plan

Square
Round

Detail of Ironwork

Detail of Column

Portico floor level

PORCH
Montrose House
PETERSHAM, SURREY
Elevation, Section and Details

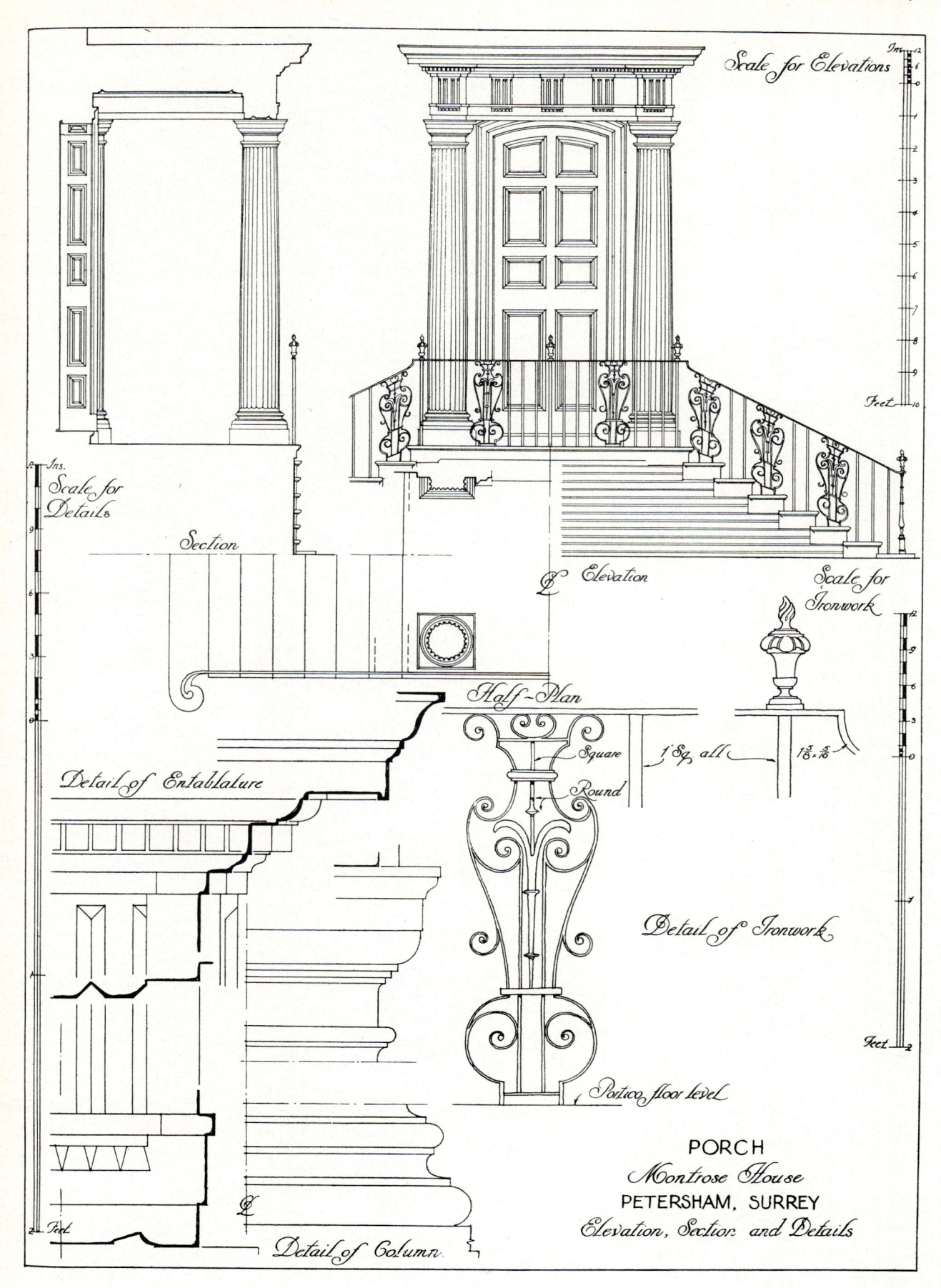

Plate 65

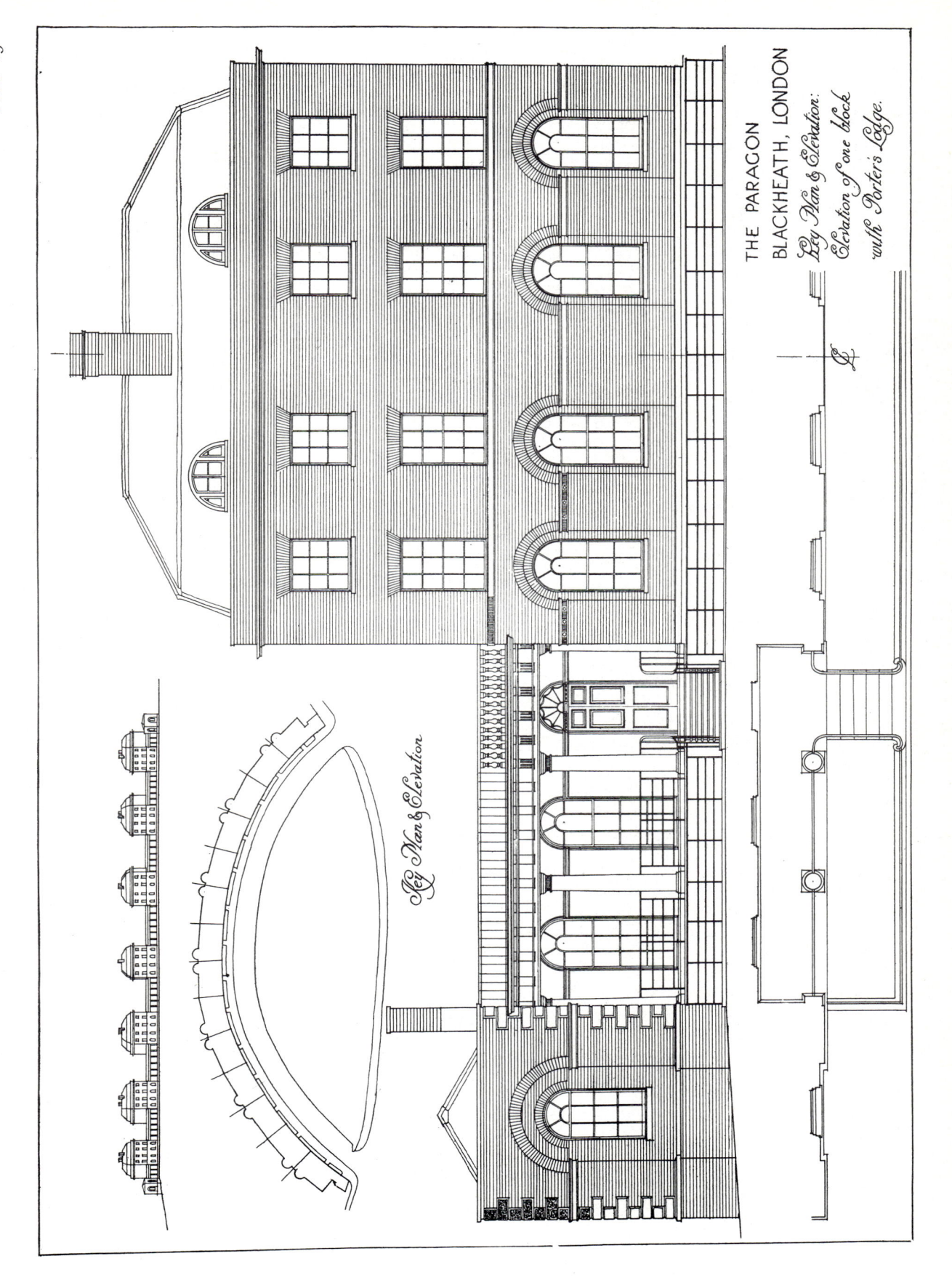

THE PARAGON
BLACKHEATH, LONDON
Key Plan & Elevation:
Elevation of one block
with Porter's Lodge.

Key Plan & Elevation

Plate 66

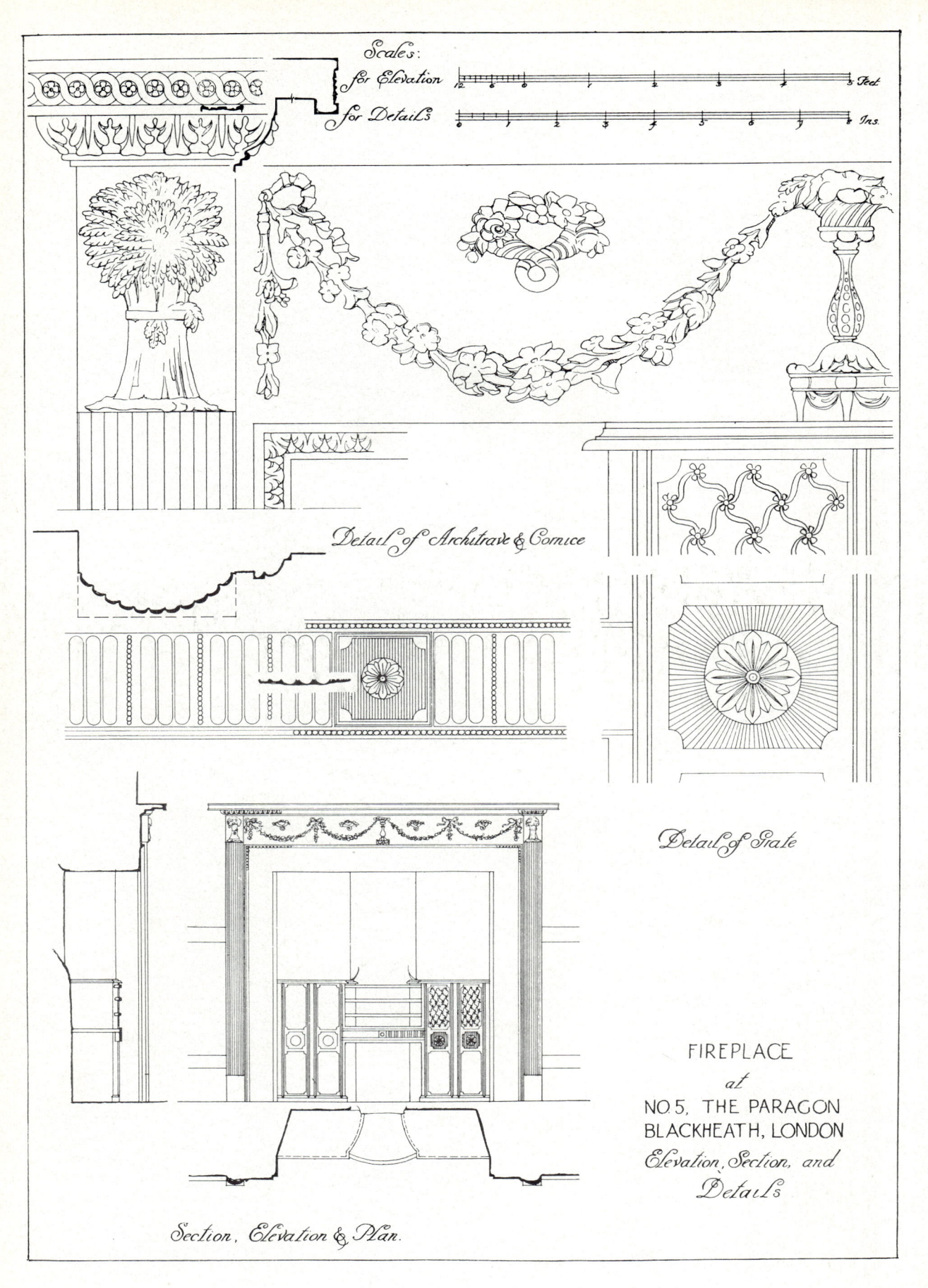

Scales:
for Elevation
for Details

Detail of Architrave & Cornice

Detail of Grate

Section, Elevation & Plan.

FIREPLACE
at
NO. 5, THE PARAGON
BLACKHEATH, LONDON
Elevation, Section, and
Details

Plate 67

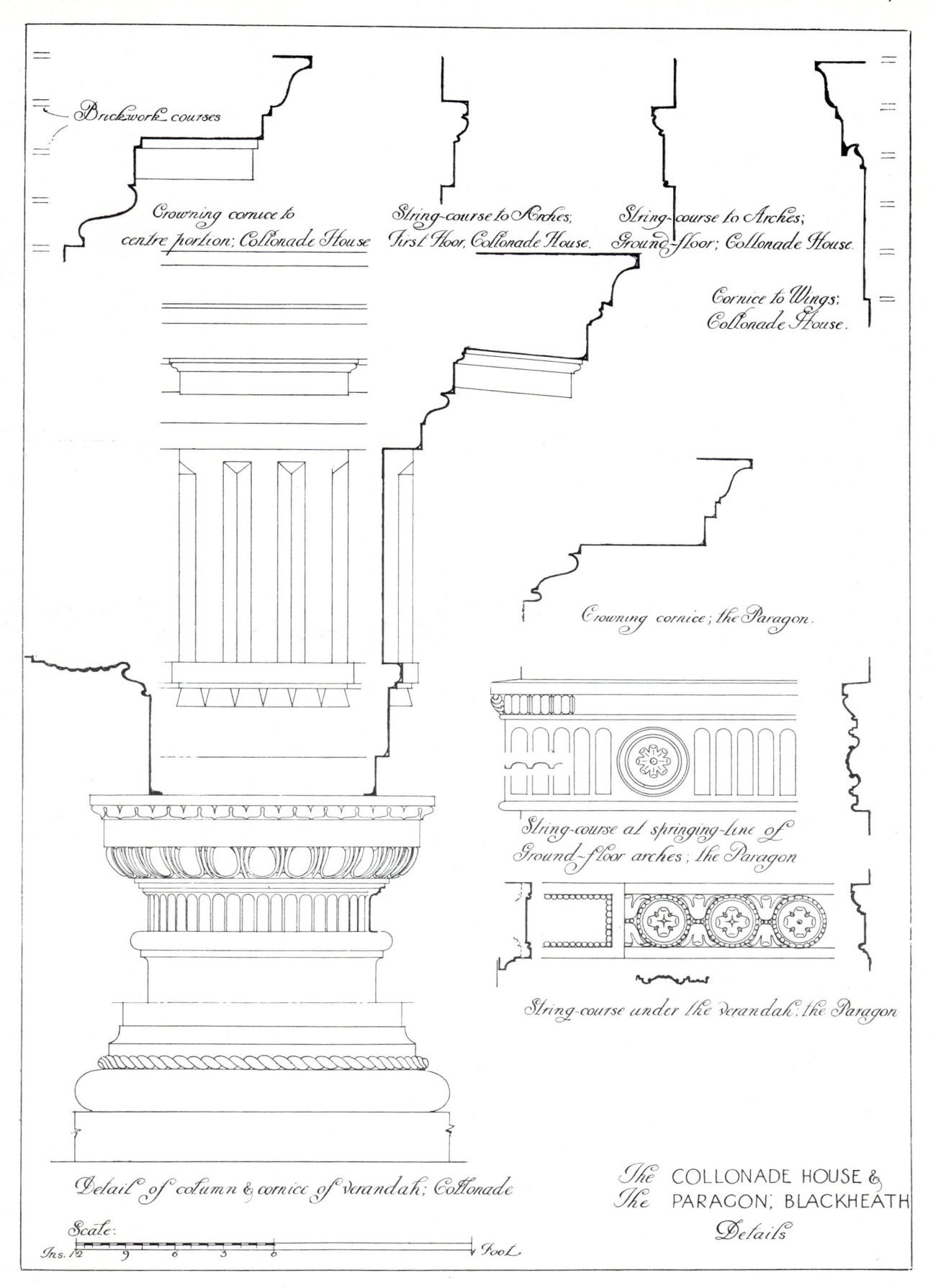

Brickwork courses

Crowning cornice to centre portion; Collonade House.

String-course to Arches; First Floor, Collonade House.

String-course to Arches; Ground-floor; Collonade House.

Cornice to Wings; Collonade House.

Crowning cornice; the Paragon.

String-course at springing-line of Ground-floor arches; the Paragon

String-course under the verandah; the Paragon

Detail of column & cornice of verandah; Collonade

Scale:
Ins. 12   9   6   3   0   Foot

The COLLONADE HOUSE &
The PARAGON; BLACKHEATH
Details

Plate 68

Elevation of Entrance Front

Plan

COLONNADE HOUSE, BLACKHEATH,
London, S.E.   Elevation

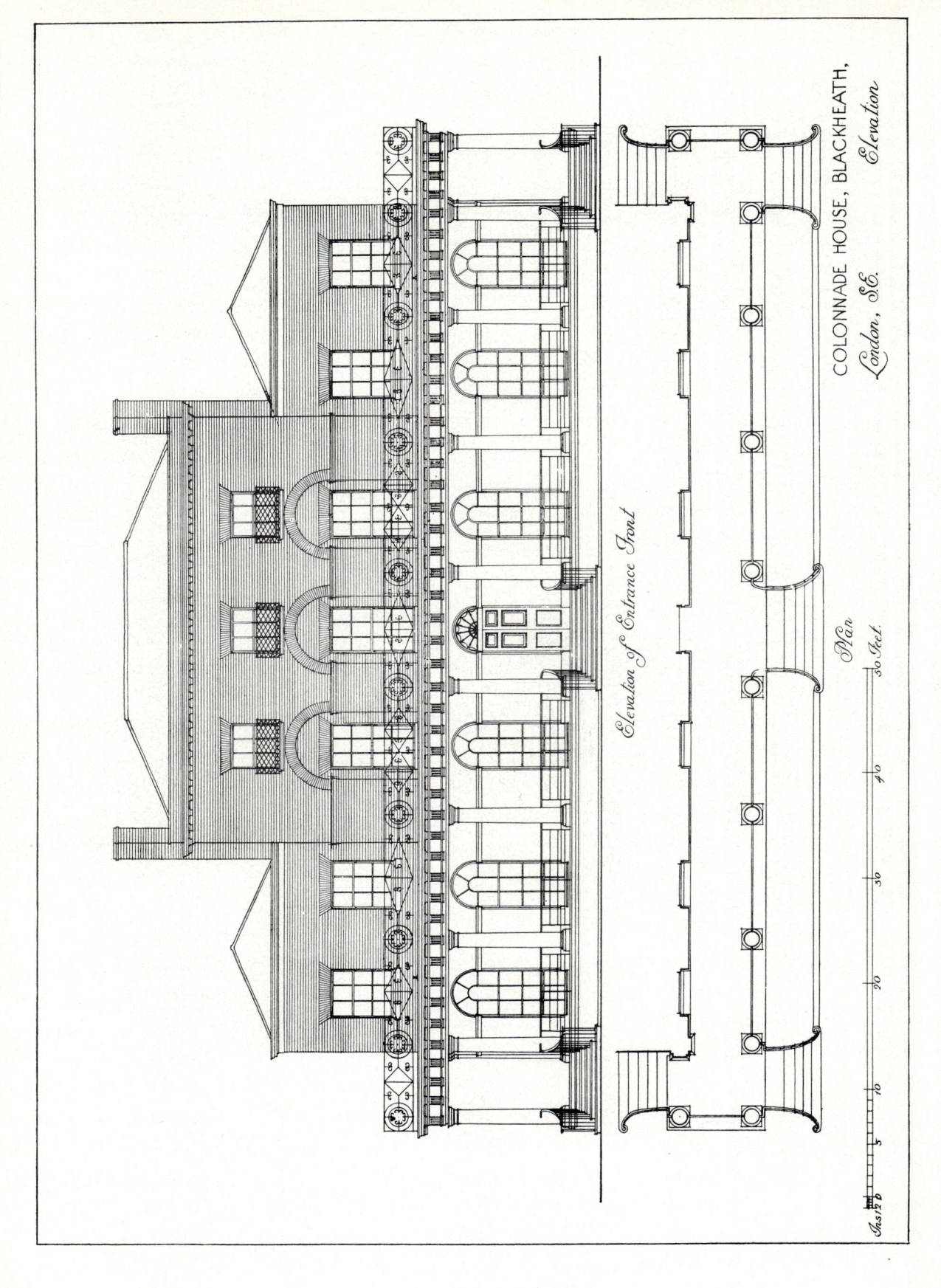

Plate 69

Front Elevation

Plan

Scale

SURREY LODGE
Denmark Hill
LONDON, S.E.
Elevation

Plate 70

Cornice to central portion

Cornice to wings

Detail of Order to Portico with pedestal.

Half plan of cap.

Order to Ground-floor windows

Repeat patera over column shown above

Transom over front door

Front door panels

Vase from No. 158. Denmark Hill

Scale for Order, etc.

Scale for Transom

SURREY LODGE
Denmark Hill.
LONDON. S.E.
Details.

Plate 71

Front Elevation

Section

Plan

Scale
Ins. 12 0 1 2 3 4 5 6 7 8 9 10   20 Feet

New Walk

Modern Sash

Mirror

HOUSE in WELL WALK,
HAMPSTEAD, LONDON
Plan, Section and Elevation
of Entrance Front.

Plate 72

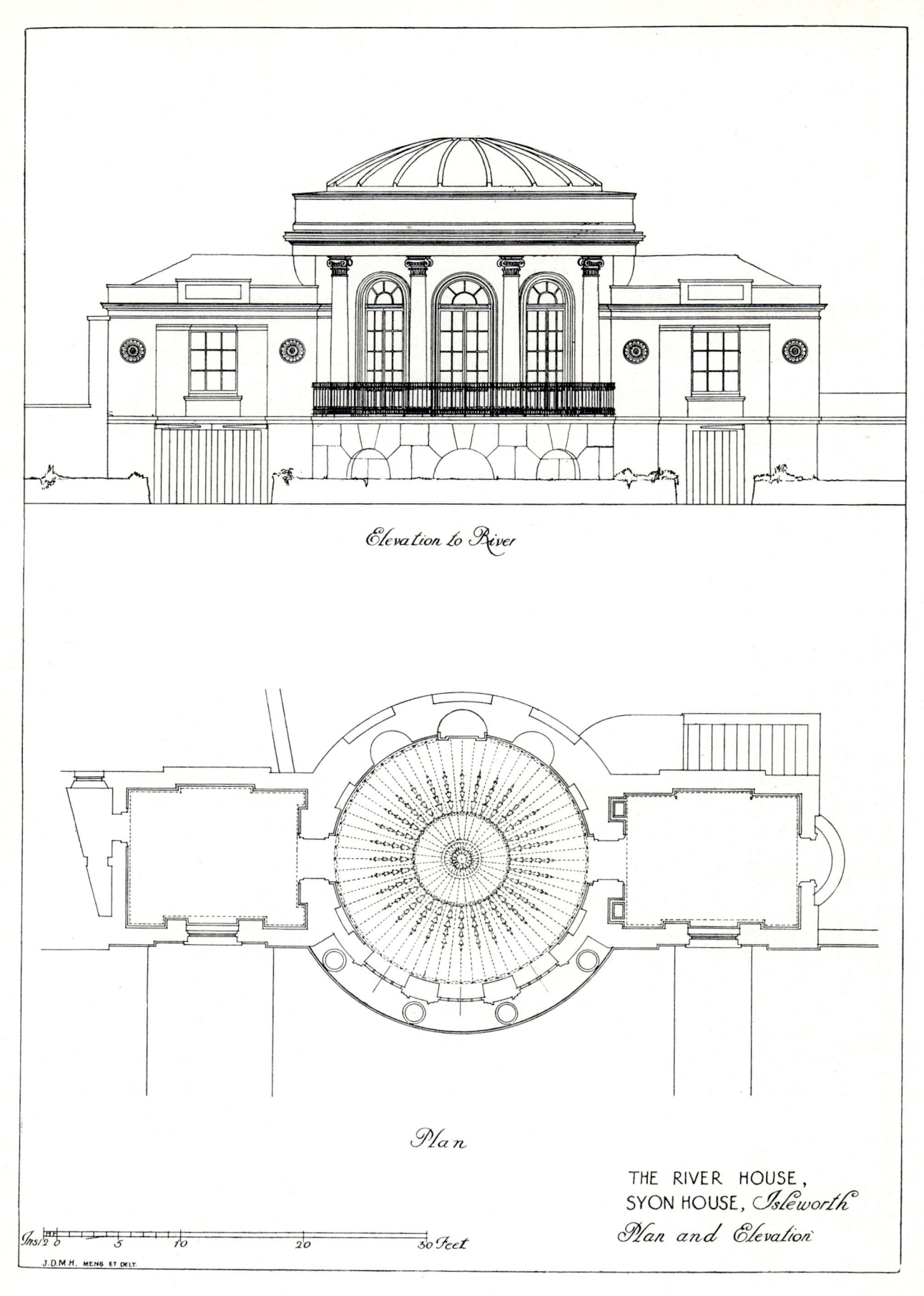

Elevation to River

Plan

THE RIVER HOUSE,
SYON HOUSE, *Isleworth*
Plan and Elevation

Ins/2 0 5 10 20 30 Feet

J.D.M.H. MENS ET DELT.

Plate 73

Longitudinal Section

Scale for section:

Main External Order

Section thro. head & panel mould of Door shown above

Cornice, dado & skirting of Circular Room.

Detail of cornice and paterae on wings

Scale for Details (Internal)
Scale for Details (External)

THE RIVER HOUSE
SYON HOUSE *Isleworth*:
Section & Details

Plate 74

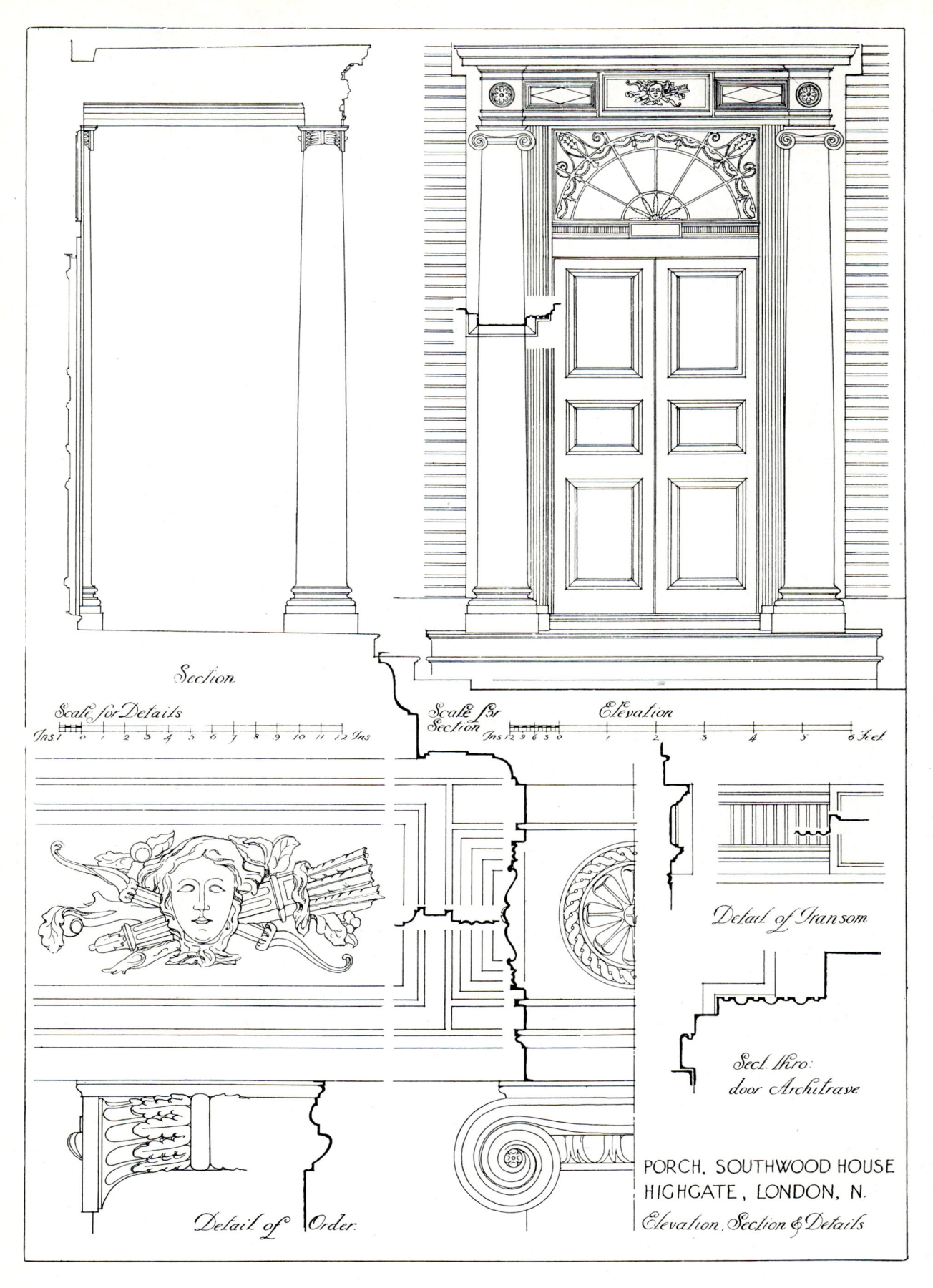

Section

Scale for Details

Scale for Section

Elevation

Detail of Transom

Sect. thro: door Architrave

Detail of Order.

PORCH, SOUTHWOOD HOUSE
HIGHGATE, LONDON, N.
Elevation, Section & Details

Plate 75

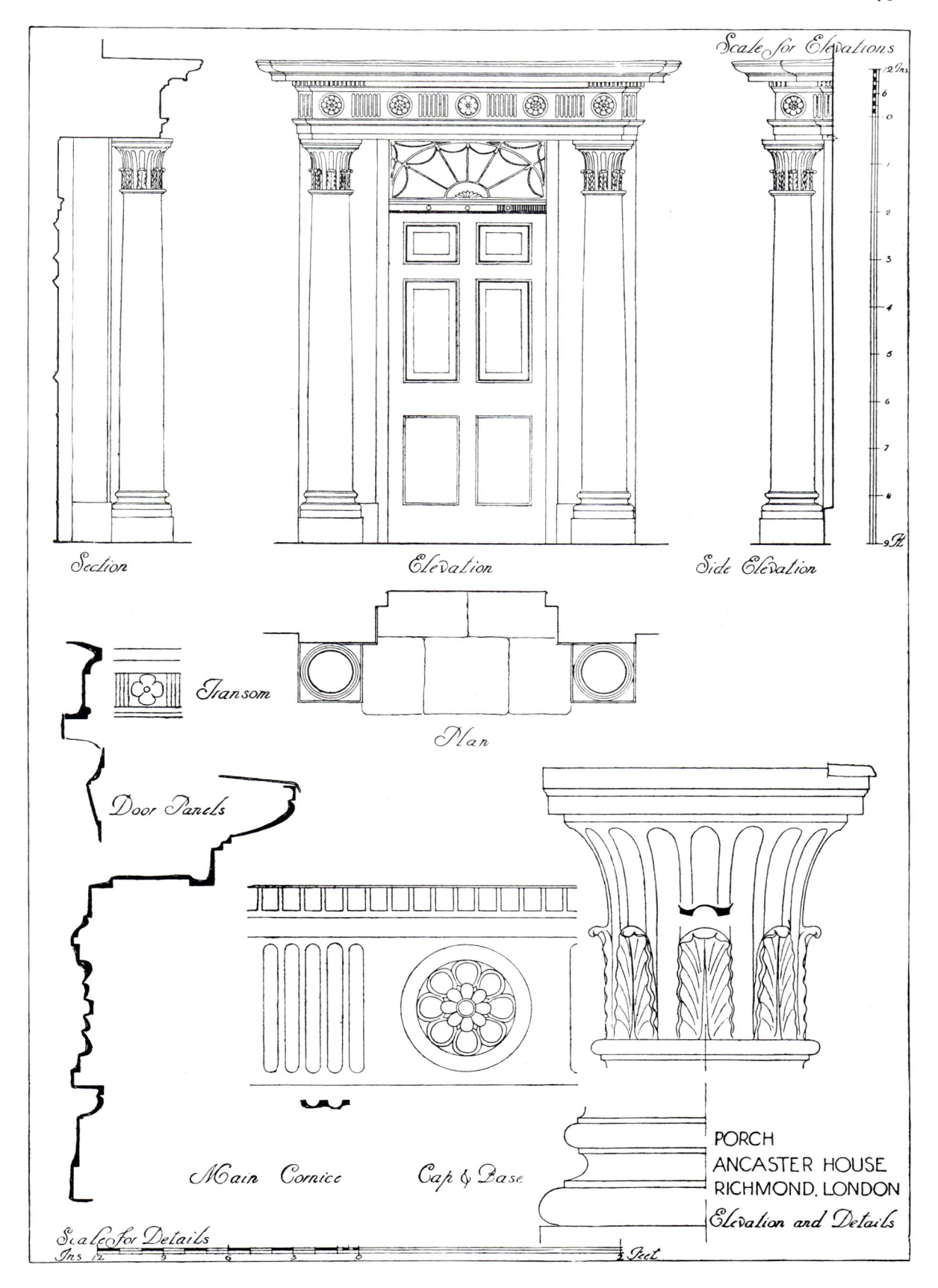

Scale for Elevations

Section   Elevation   Side Elevation

Transom

Plan

Door Panels

Main Cornice   Cap & Base

PORCH
ANCASTER HOUSE
RICHMOND, LONDON
Elevation and Details

Scale for Details

Plate 76

Section

Elevation

Section thro' Head at "D"

Plan

Plan at Angle "A"

TRELLIS PORCH
"The Limes"
KINGSTON-ON-THAMES
Plan, Section, Elevation
and Details.

Scale for Elevations.
Scale for Details.

Plate 77

Section

Elevation

Cap & Cornice

Panel moulding

Half-Plan

DOORWAY & BALCONY,
UPPER KENNINGTON LANE,
LONDON. S.E.
Elevation and Details

Scale for Elevation
Scale for Details

Plate 78

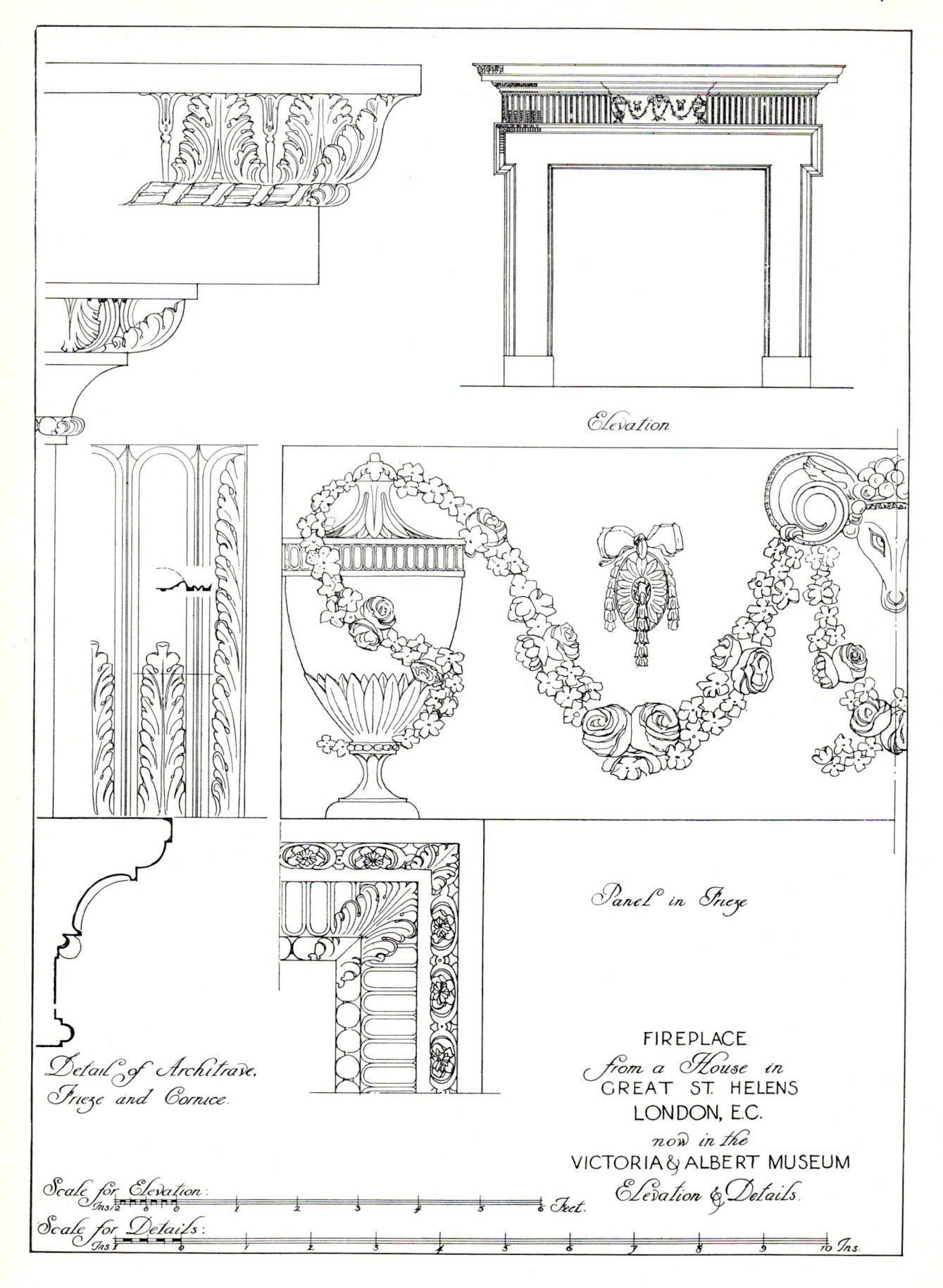

Elevation

Panel in Frieze

Detail of Architrave, Frieze and Cornice.

FIREPLACE
from a House in
GREAT ST. HELENS
LONDON, E.C.
now in the
VICTORIA & ALBERT MUSEUM
Elevation & Details.

Scale for Elevation:
Scale for Details:

Plate 79

Detail of Order, Panel in Freize, and Architrave around the Fireplace Opening.

Plan through Column and Architrave looking up.

Base of column

Elevation

FIREPLACE
in the
VICTORIA & ALBERT MUSEUM,
SOUTH KENSINGTON, LONDON.
Elevation & Details.

Scales:
for Elevation:
for Details:

Plate 80

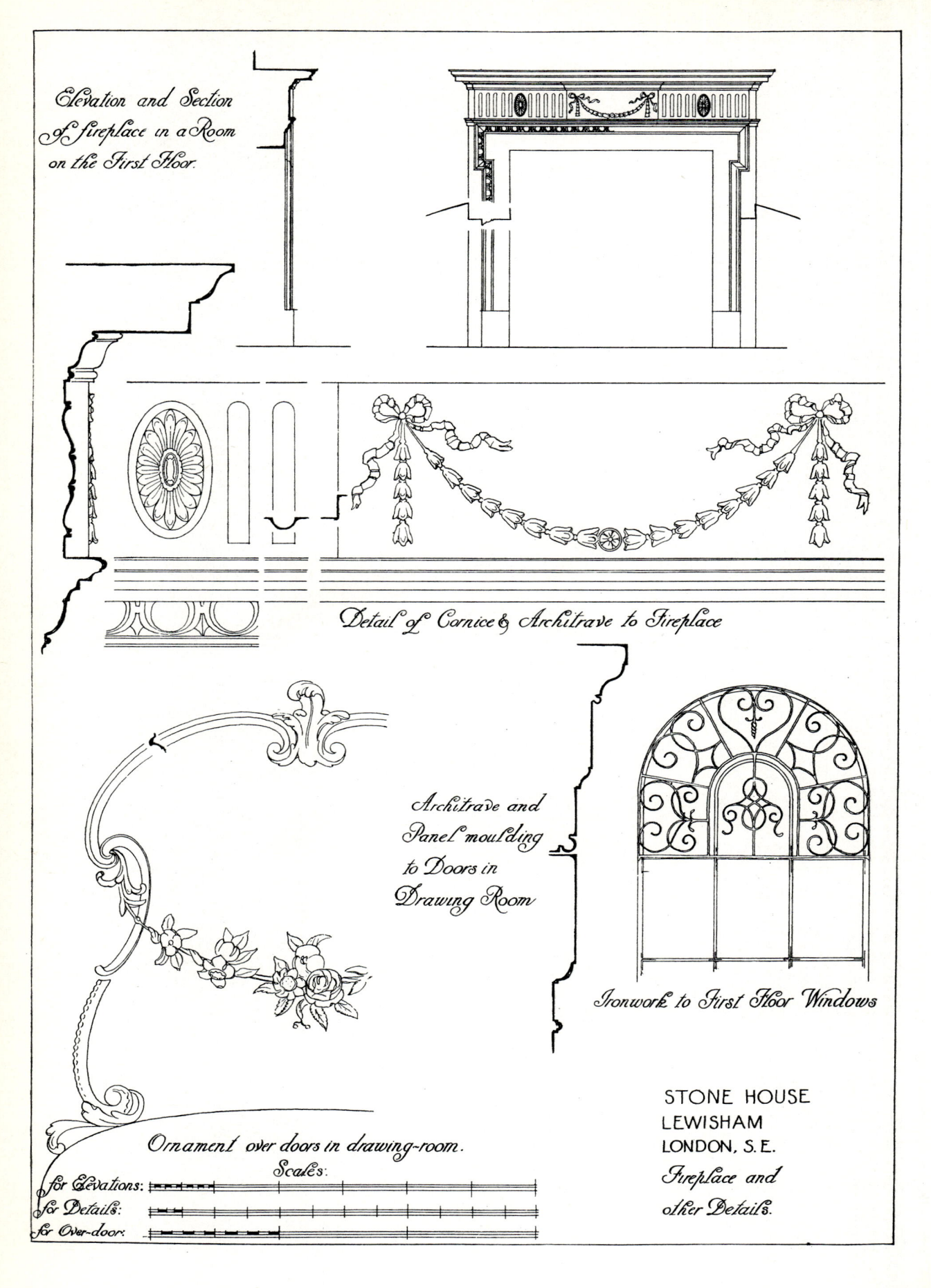

Elevation and Section of fireplace in a Room on the First Floor.

Detail of Cornice & Architrave to Fireplace

Architrave and Panel moulding to Doors in Drawing Room

Ironwork to First Floor Windows

Ornament over doors in drawing-room.

Scales:
for Elevations:
for Details:
for Over-door:

STONE HOUSE
LEWISHAM
LONDON, S.E.
Fireplace and other Details.

Plate 81

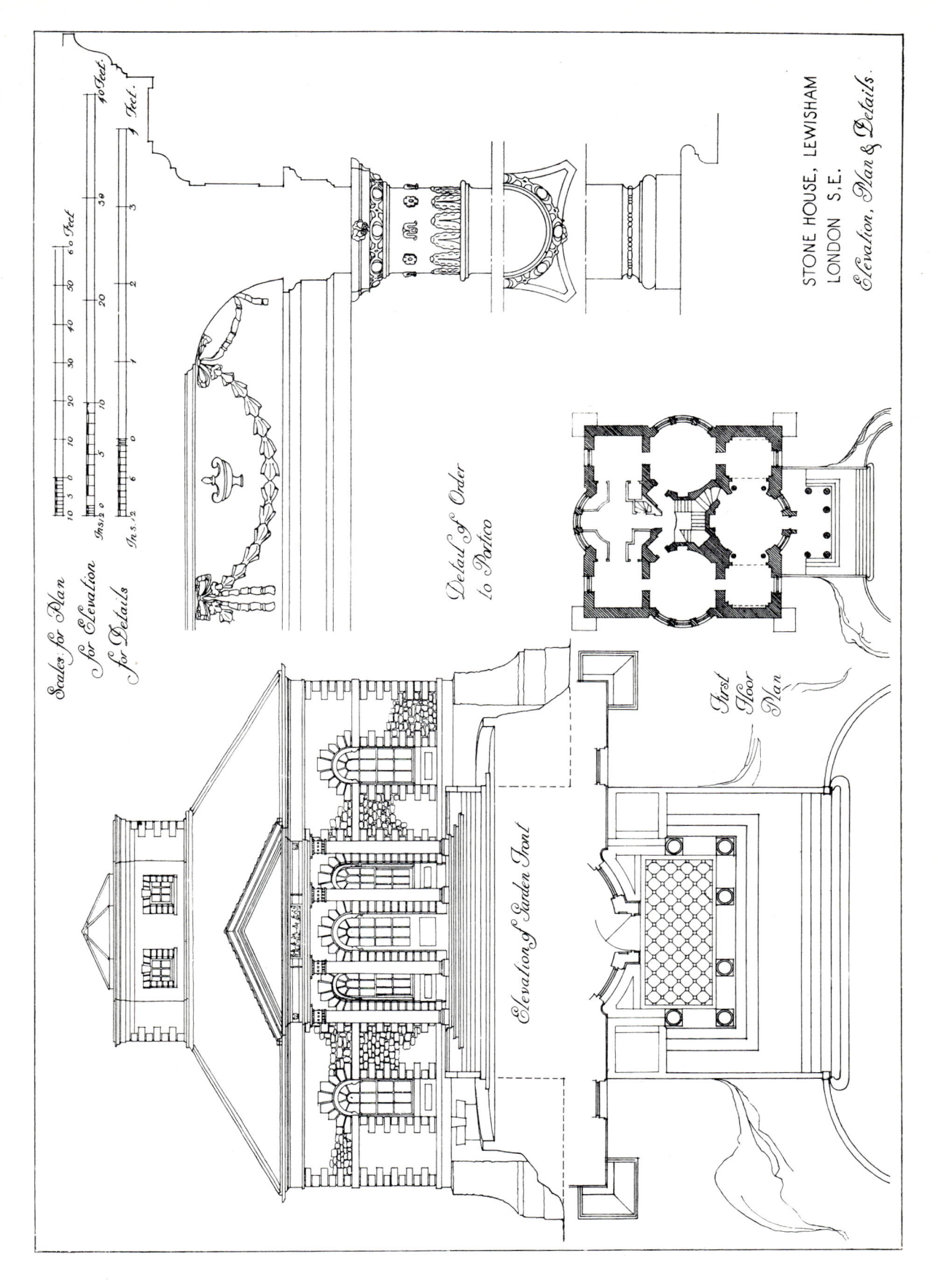

STONE HOUSE, LEWISHAM
LONDON S.E.
Elevation, Plan & Details.

Scales for Plan
for Elevation
for Details

Detail of Order to Portico

First Floor Plan

Elevation of Garden Front

Plate 82

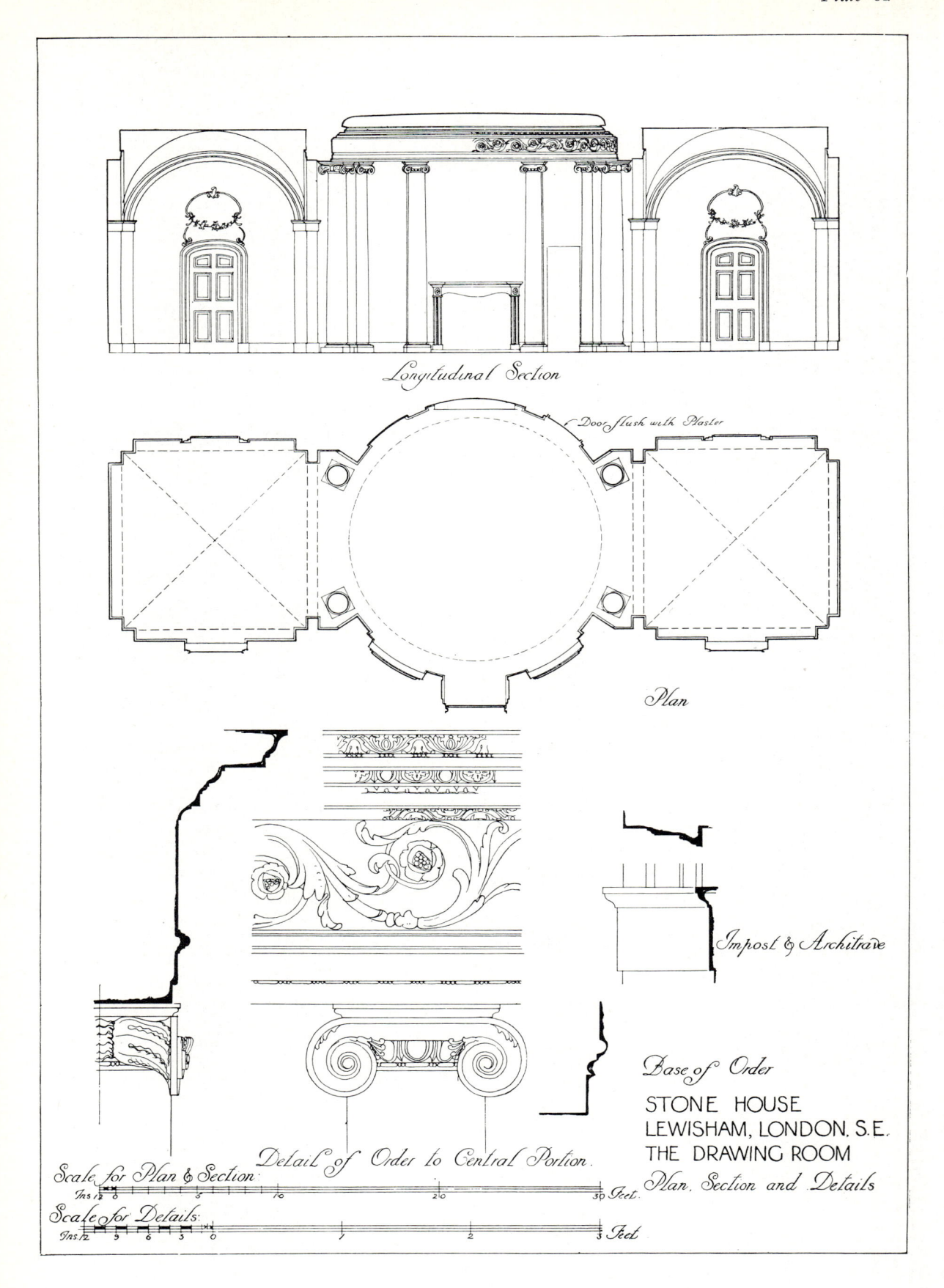

Longitudinal Section

Door flush with Plaster

Plan

Impost & Architrave

Base of Order

Detail of Order to Central Portion.

STONE HOUSE
LEWISHAM, LONDON, S.E.
THE DRAWING ROOM
Plan, Section and Details

Scale for Plan & Section:
Scale for Details:

Plate 83

Elevation to River.

KENT HOUSE
Lower Mall, Hammersmith
LONDON, W.
Elevation of Entrance Front.

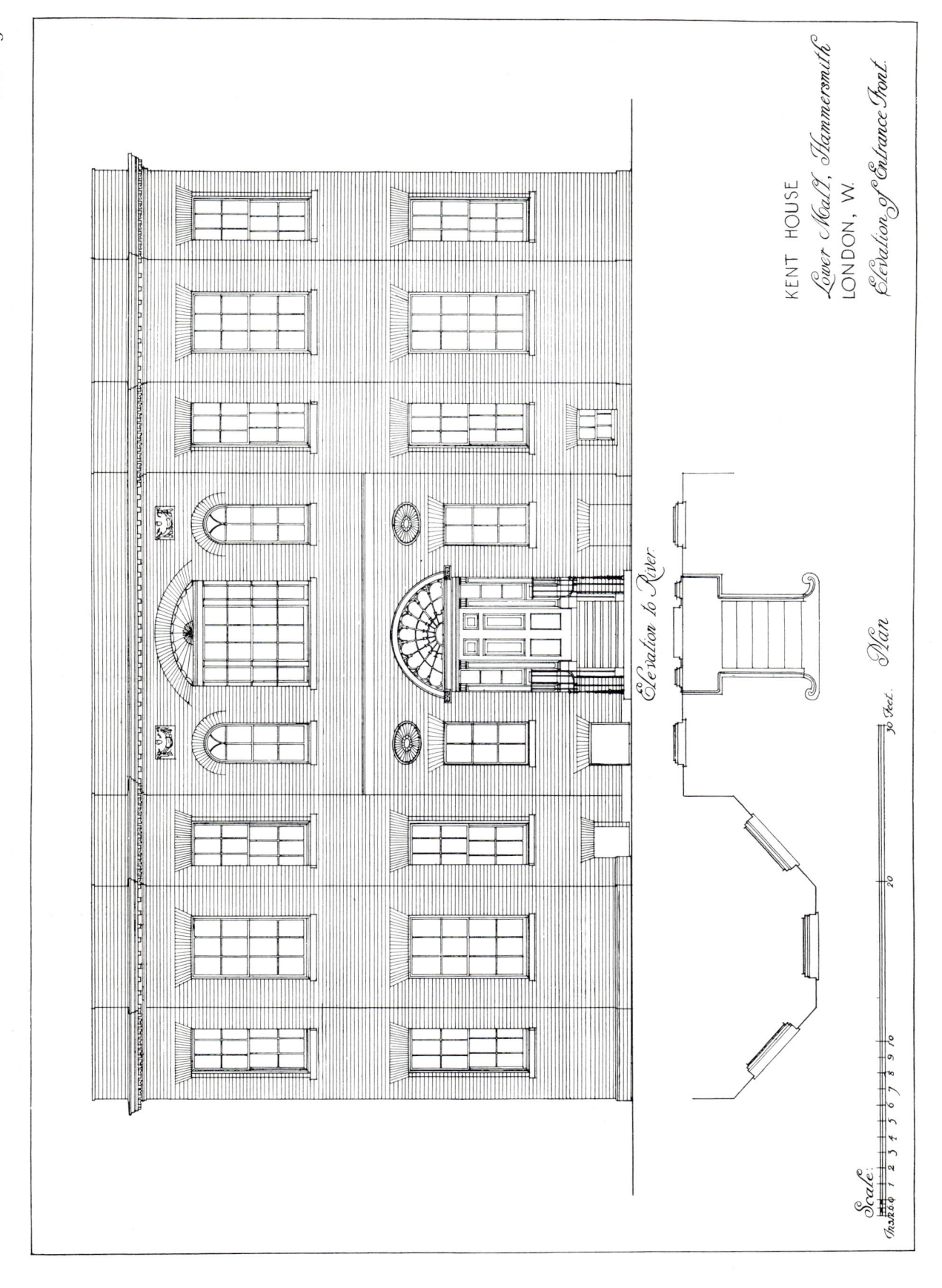

Scale: 1 2 3 4 5 6 7 8 9 10   20   30 feet.   Plan.

Plate 84

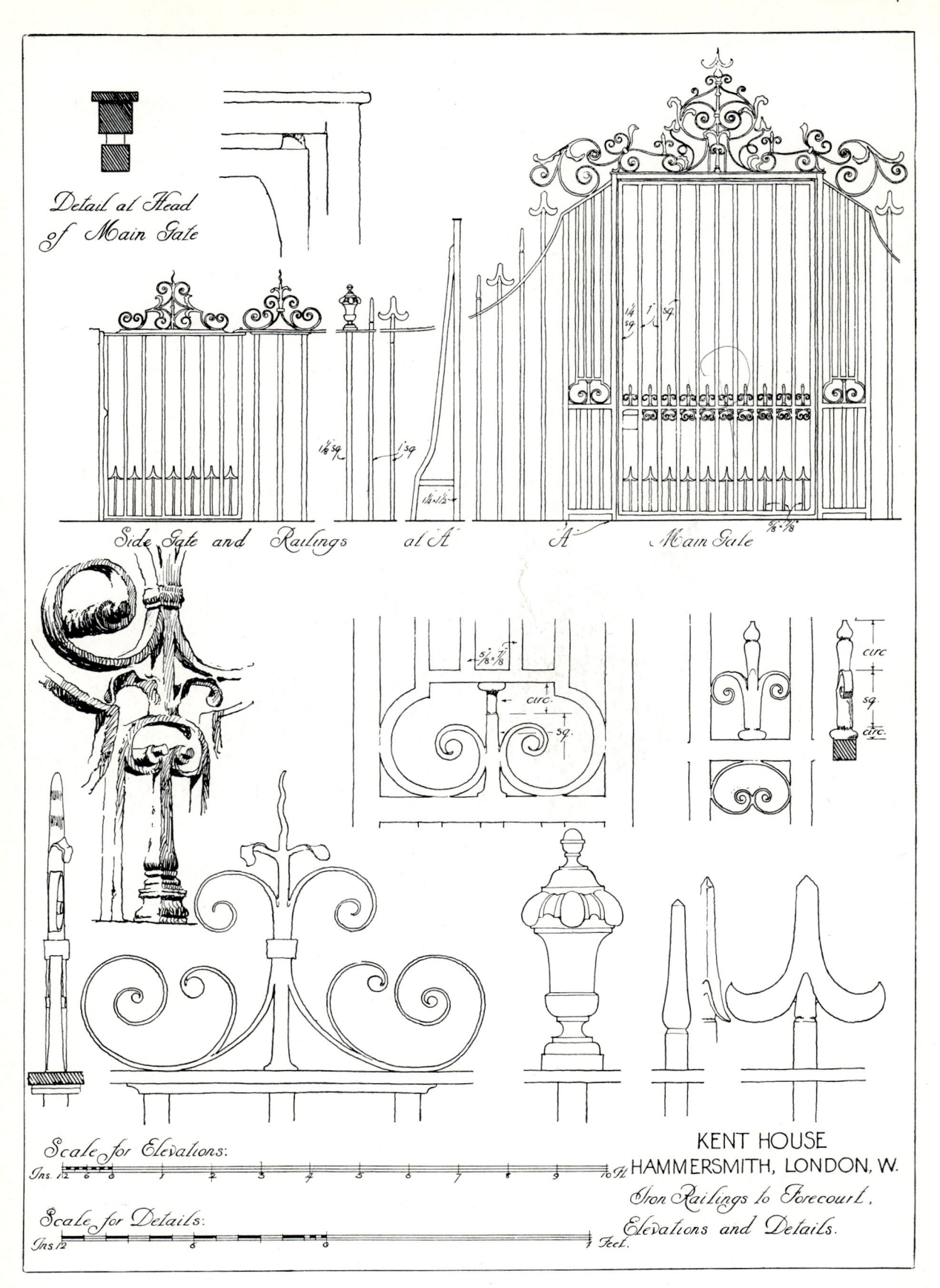

Detail at Head of Main Gate

Side Gate and Railings at "A"   "A"   Main Gate

Scale for Elevations:
Ins.

Scale for Details:
Ins.

KENT HOUSE
HAMMERSMITH, LONDON, W.
Iron Railings to Forecourt,
Elevations and Details.

Plate 85

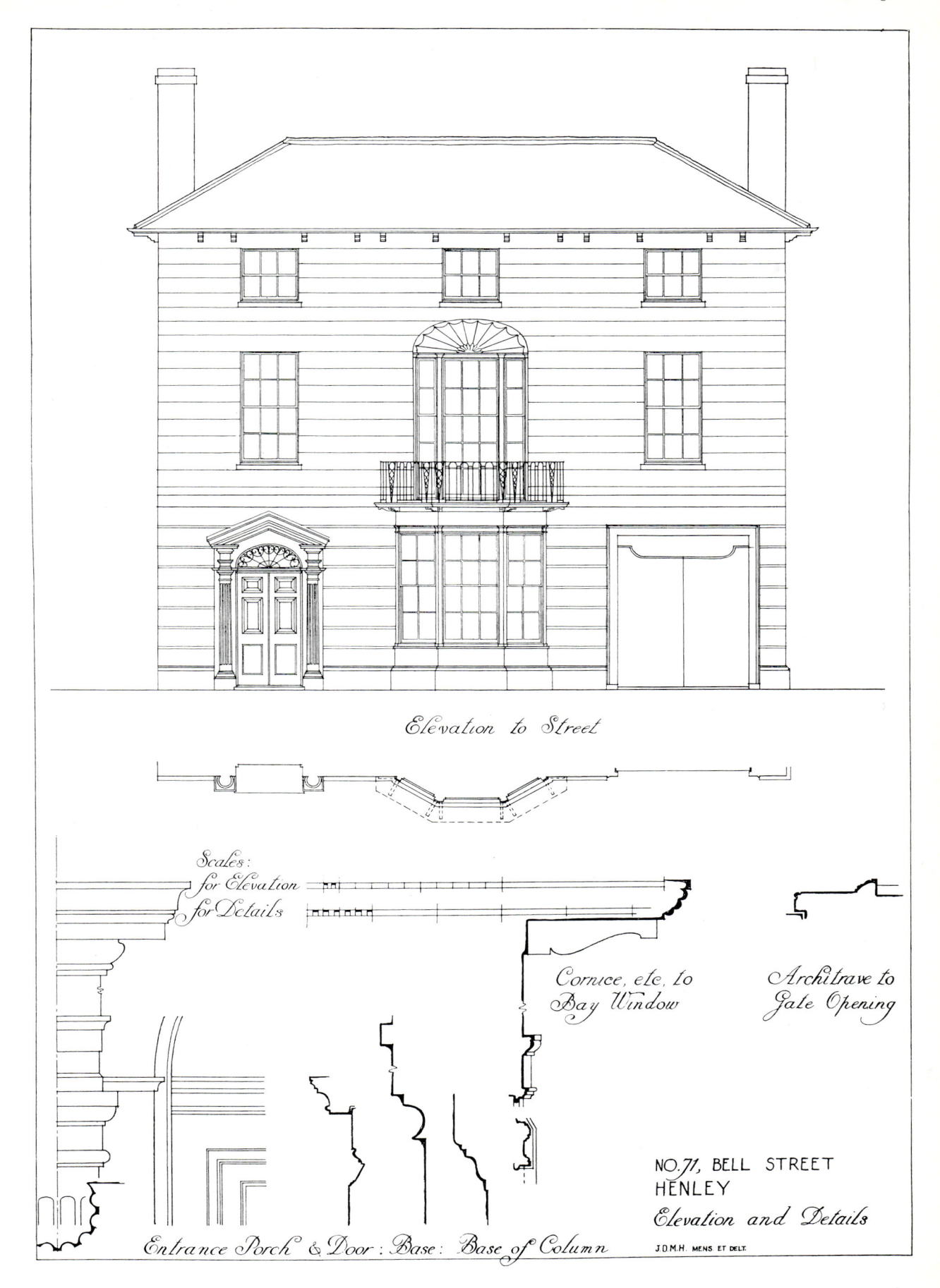

Elevation to Street

Scales:
for Elevation
for Details

Cornice, etc, to Bay Window

Architrave to Gate Opening

Entrance Porch & Door : Base : Base of Column

NO. 71, BELL STREET
HENLEY
Elevation and Details

J.D.M.H. MENS. ET DELT.

Plate 86

"THE WICK" RICHMOND, SURREY
Elevation of Entrance Front

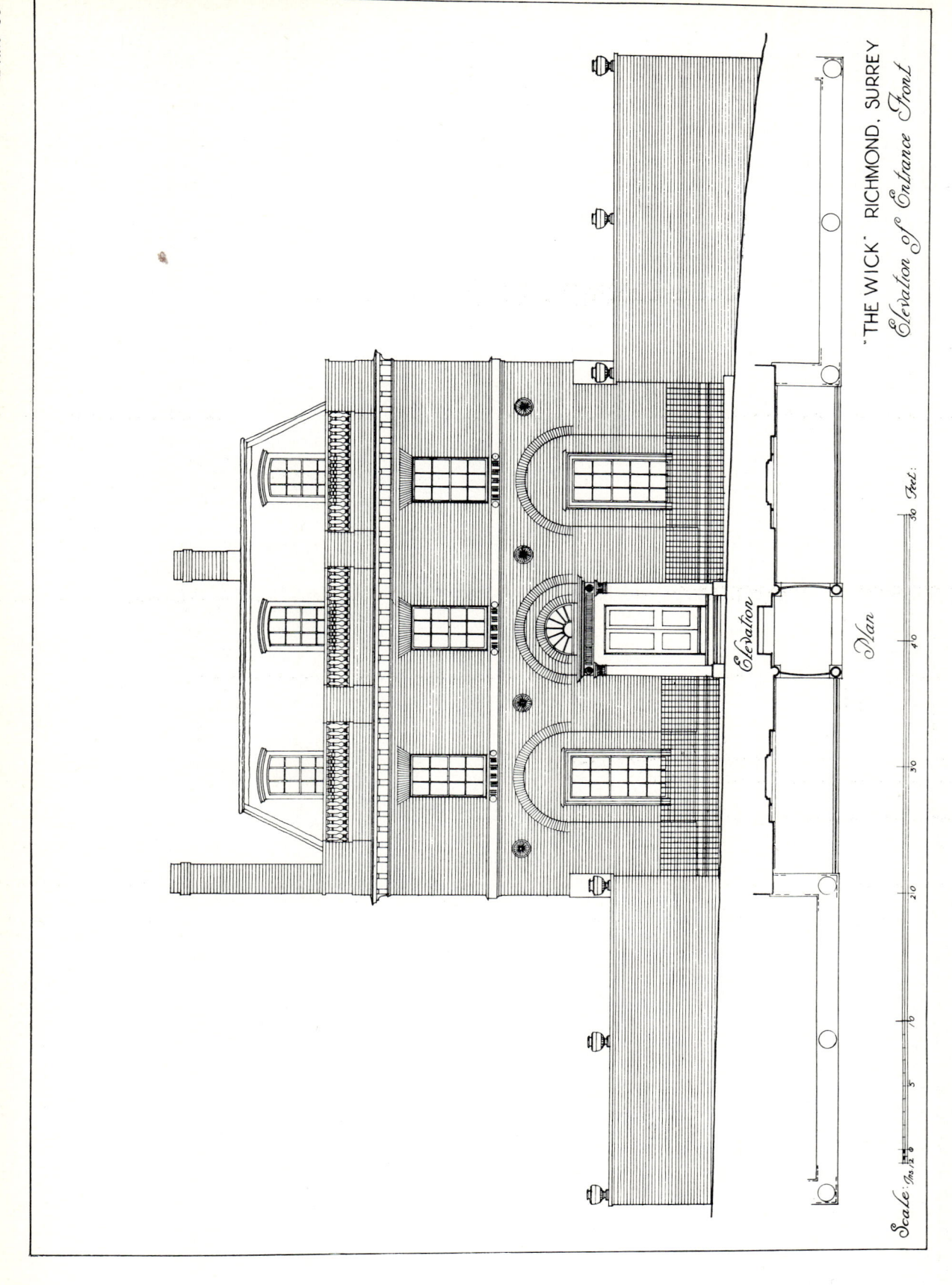

Plate 87

Scale

Main Cornice

String-course under
First-floor windows

Detail of Order to Portico

Medallions over Piers

String-course at
Ground Floor Level

Vase on Wing Walls

THE WICK
RICHMOND SURREY
Details of Entrance Front

Plate 88

ENSLEIGH LODGE
HAM COMMON, SURREY
Elevation of Entrance Front

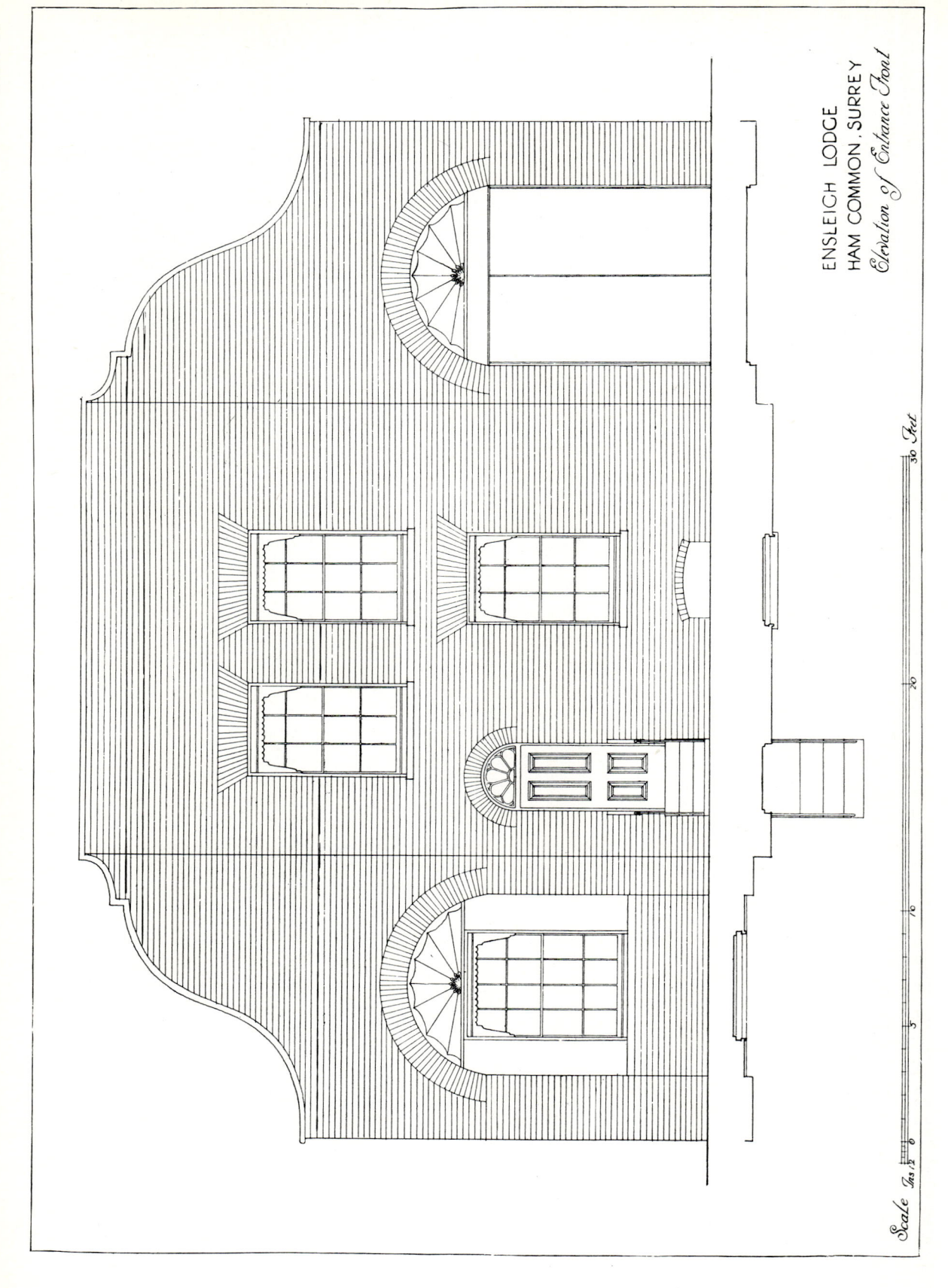

Scale Ins. 12 6   5   10   20   30 Feet

Plate 89

THORNCROFT MANOR,
LEATHERHEAD, SURREY.
Elevation of Entrance Front.

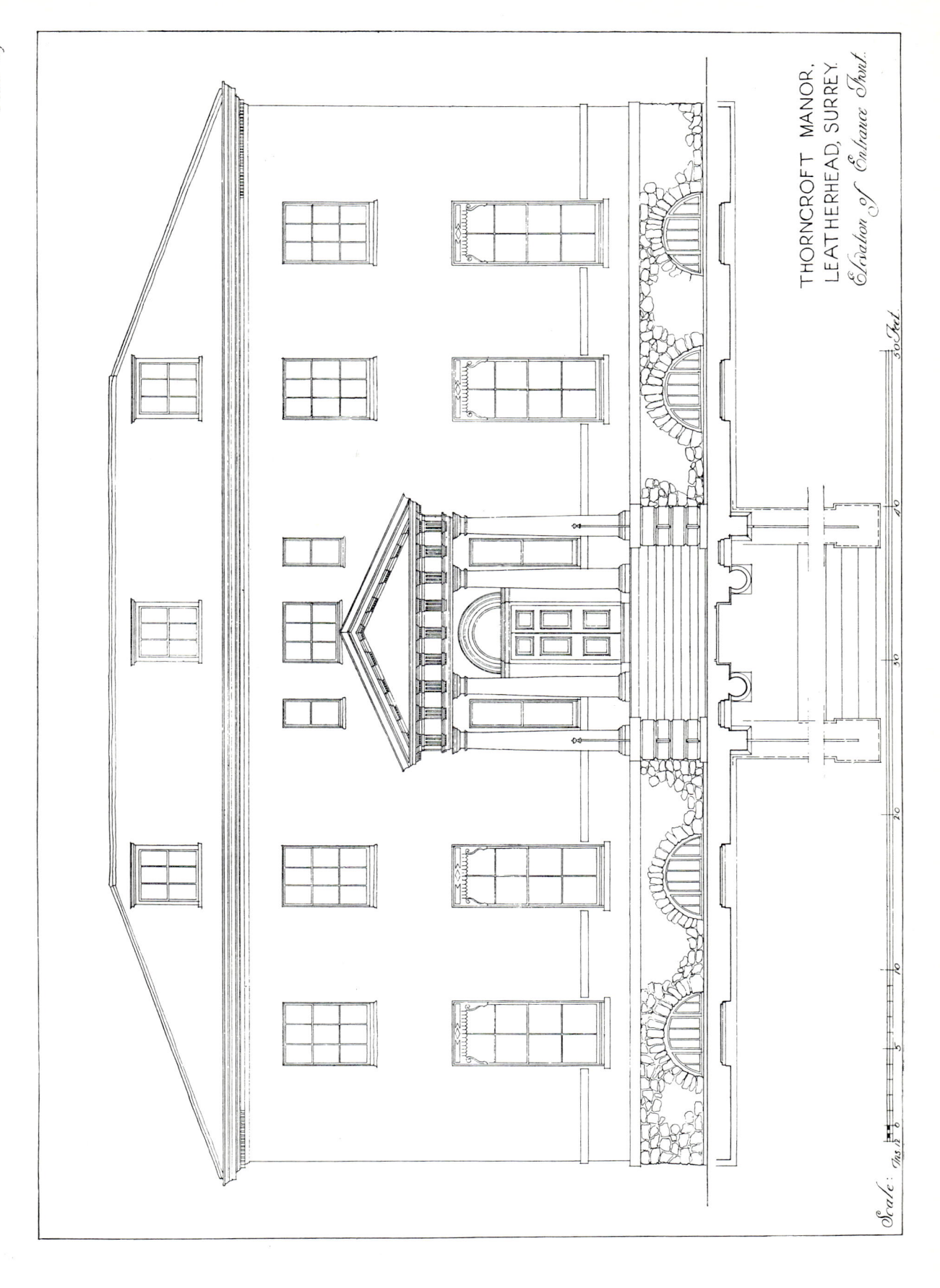

Scale: Ins. 3   5   10   20   30   40   50 Feet

Plate 90

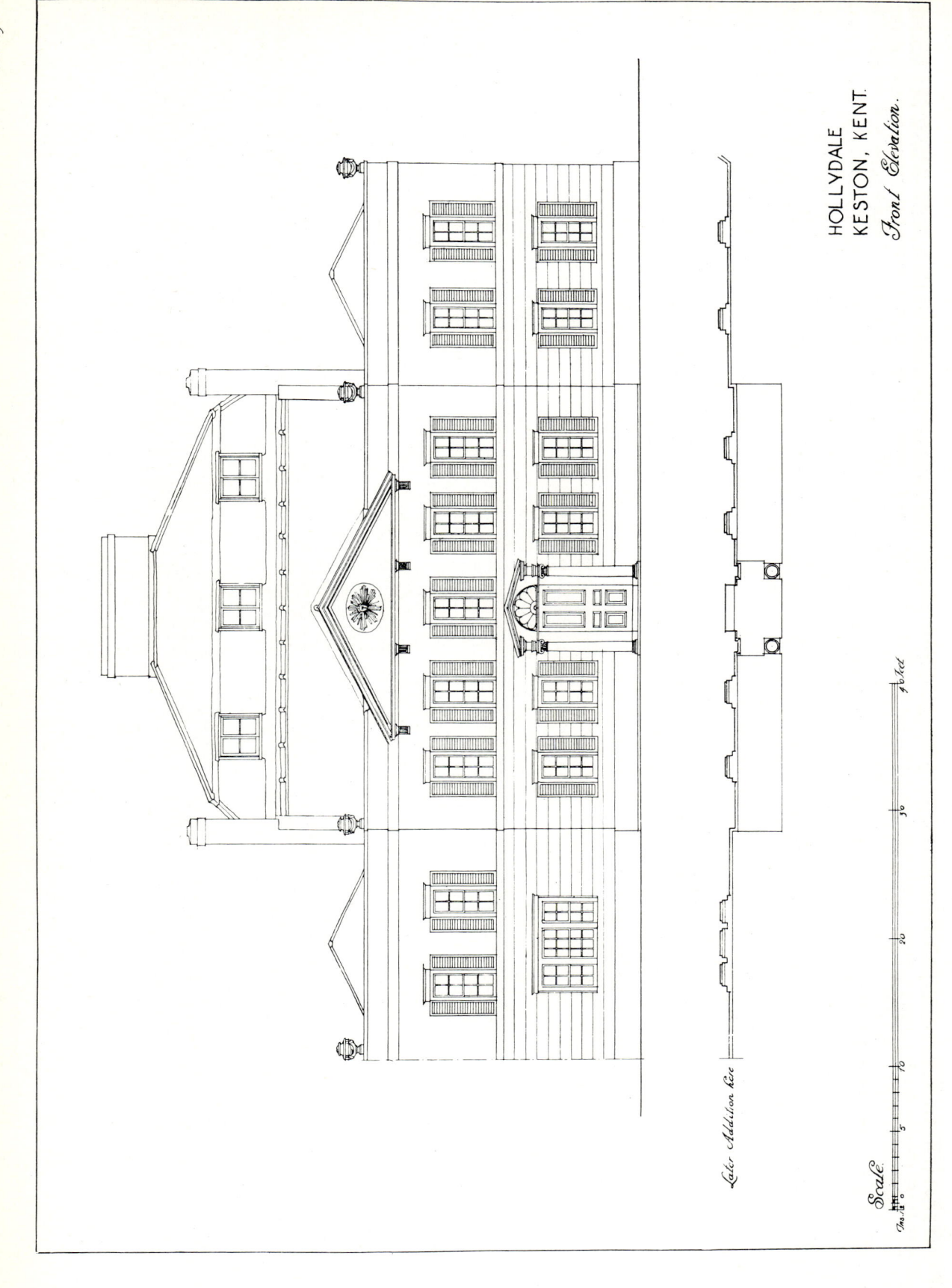

HOLLYDALE
KESTON, KENT.
Front Elevation.

Scale.

Later Addition &c

Plate 91

Elevation of Dining-room Bay.

Detail of bracket and Pediment on Front Elevation

♃ of column and Pilaster

♃ of bracket

Pilaster to Entrance

Detail of enriched band over windows

Detail of columns of Portico on Entrance Front

Vases on Front & Side Elevations.

Panel over Windows.

"HOLLYDALE," KESTON, KENT.

Scale for Elevation:— Ins.12 0   10   20 Feet
Scale for Details:— Ins.12   6   0   1 Foot

Details

J.D.M.H. MENS ET DELT.

Plate 92

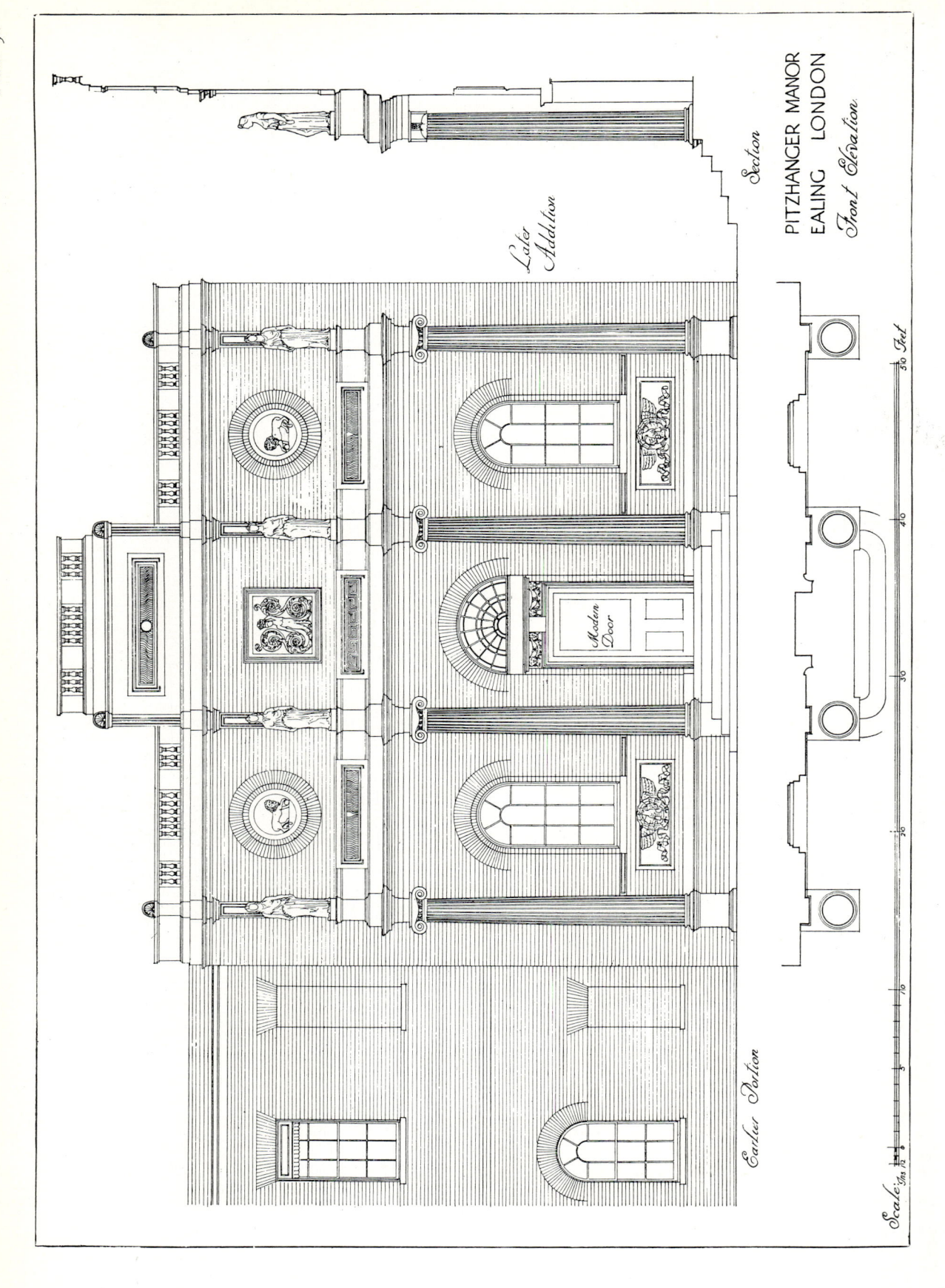

Section

Later Addition

Earlier Portion

Modern Door

Scale ⅛ in = 1 ft   0   5   10   20   30   40   50 Feet

PITZHANGER MANOR
EALING   LONDON
Front Elevation

Plate 93

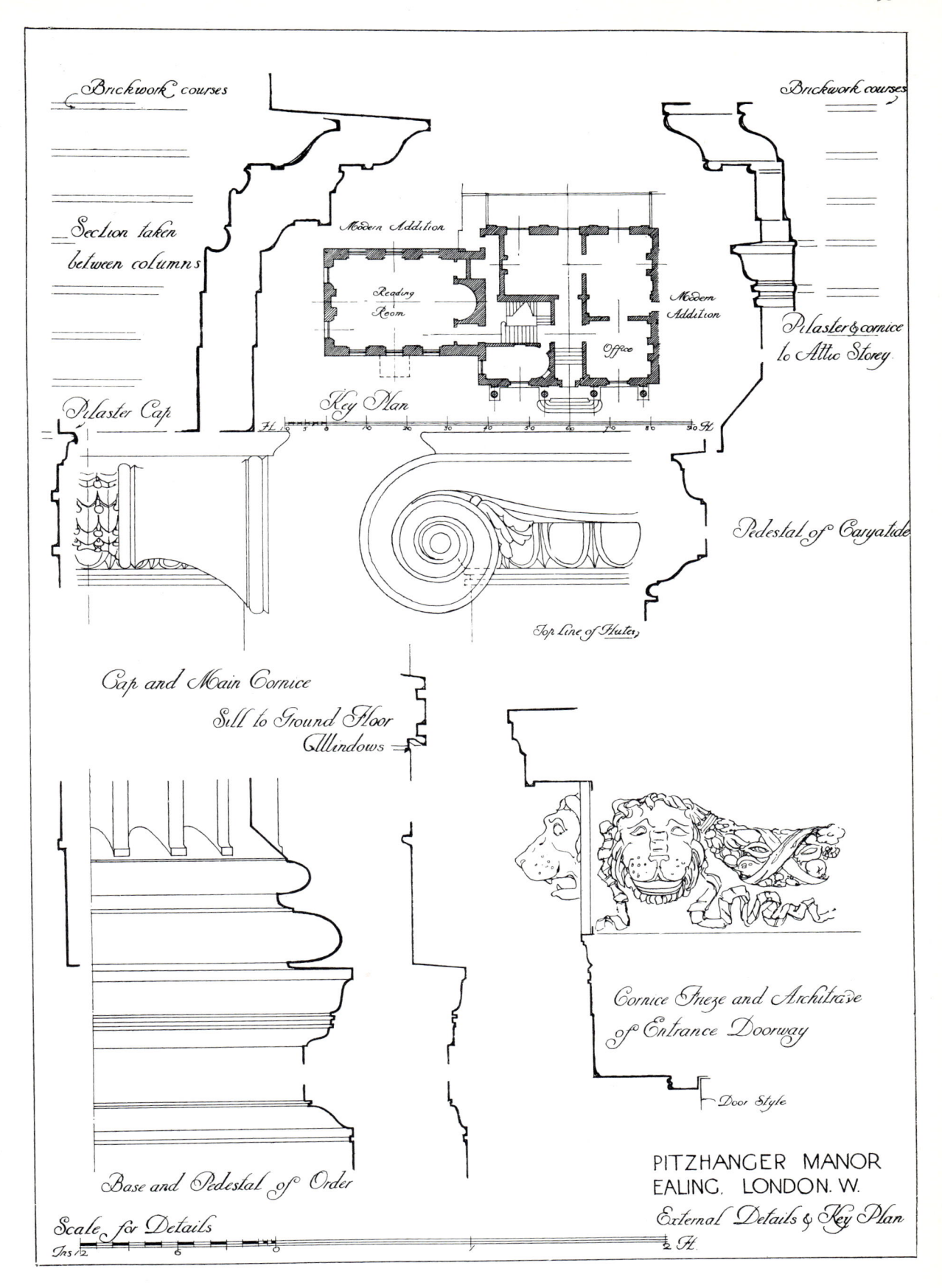

Brickwork courses

Brickwork courses

Section taken between columns

Modern Addition

Reading Room

Modern Addition

Office

Pilaster & cornice to Attic Storey

Pilaster Cap

Key Plan

Pedestal of Caryatide

Top line of Fluter

Cap and Main Cornice

Sill to Ground Floor Windows

Cornice Frieze and Architrave of Entrance Doorway

Door Style

Base and Pedestal of Order

PITZHANGER MANOR
EALING. LONDON. W.
External Details & Key Plan

Scale for Details

Plate 94

Scale for Section
Ins 12 0   5   10   20 Feet.

Elevation and part-plan of End of Room

Section through Niche

Dado

Skirting

Frieze under Springing Line of Niche.

Architrave to Doors

Panel-mould to Doors

Architrave of Niche

PITZHANGER MANOR
EALING, LONDON, W.
Reading Room
Section and Details

Scale for Details.
Ins 1 0 1 2 3 4 5 6 7 Ins.

Plate 95

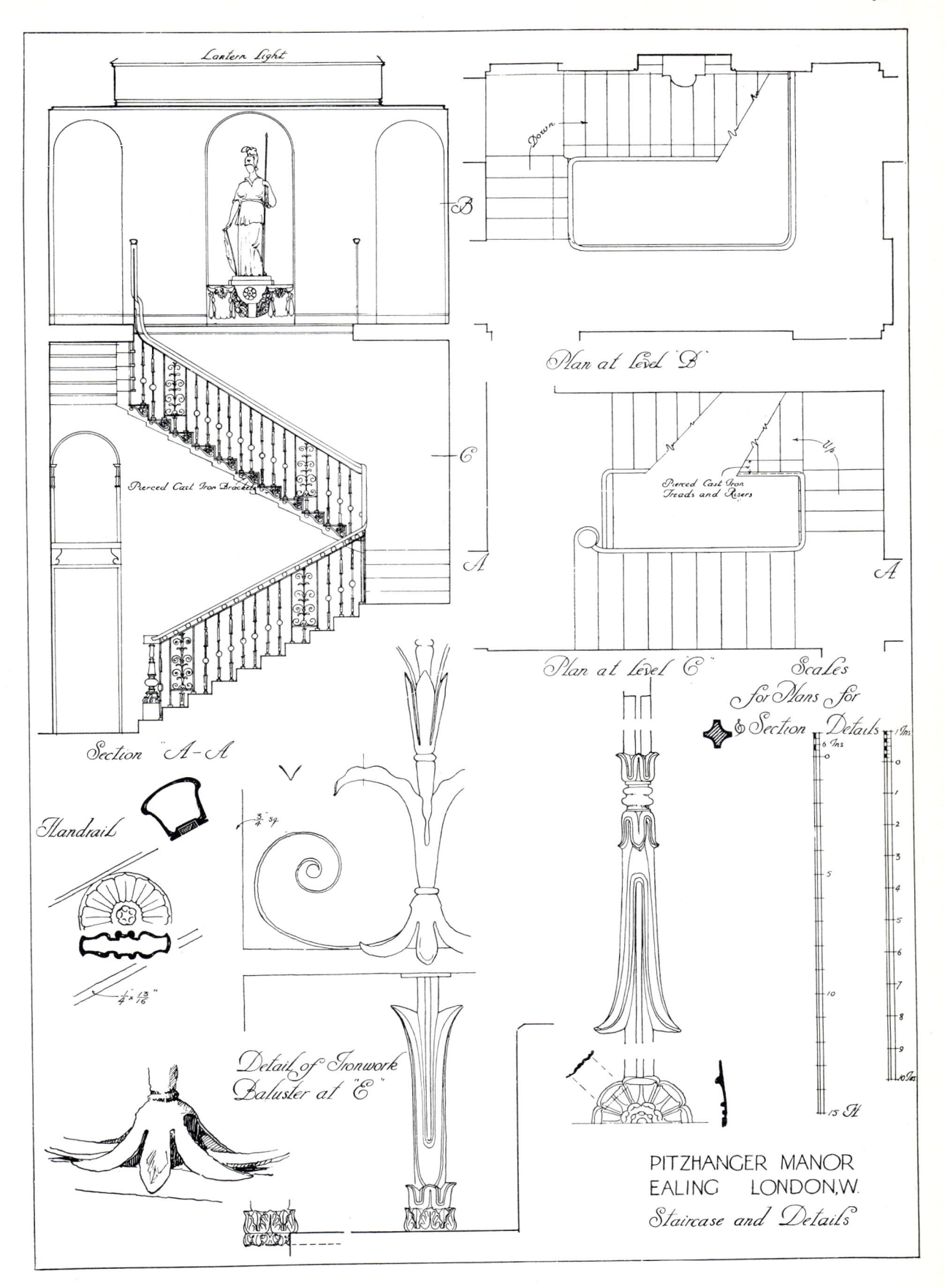

Lantern Light

Plan at level "B"

Pierced Cast Iron Brackets

Pierced Cast Iron Treads and Risers

Section "A-A"

Plan at level "C"

Handrail

Scales for Plans for Section Details

Detail of Ironwork Baluster at "E"

PITZHANGER MANOR
EALING LONDON, W.
Staircase and Details

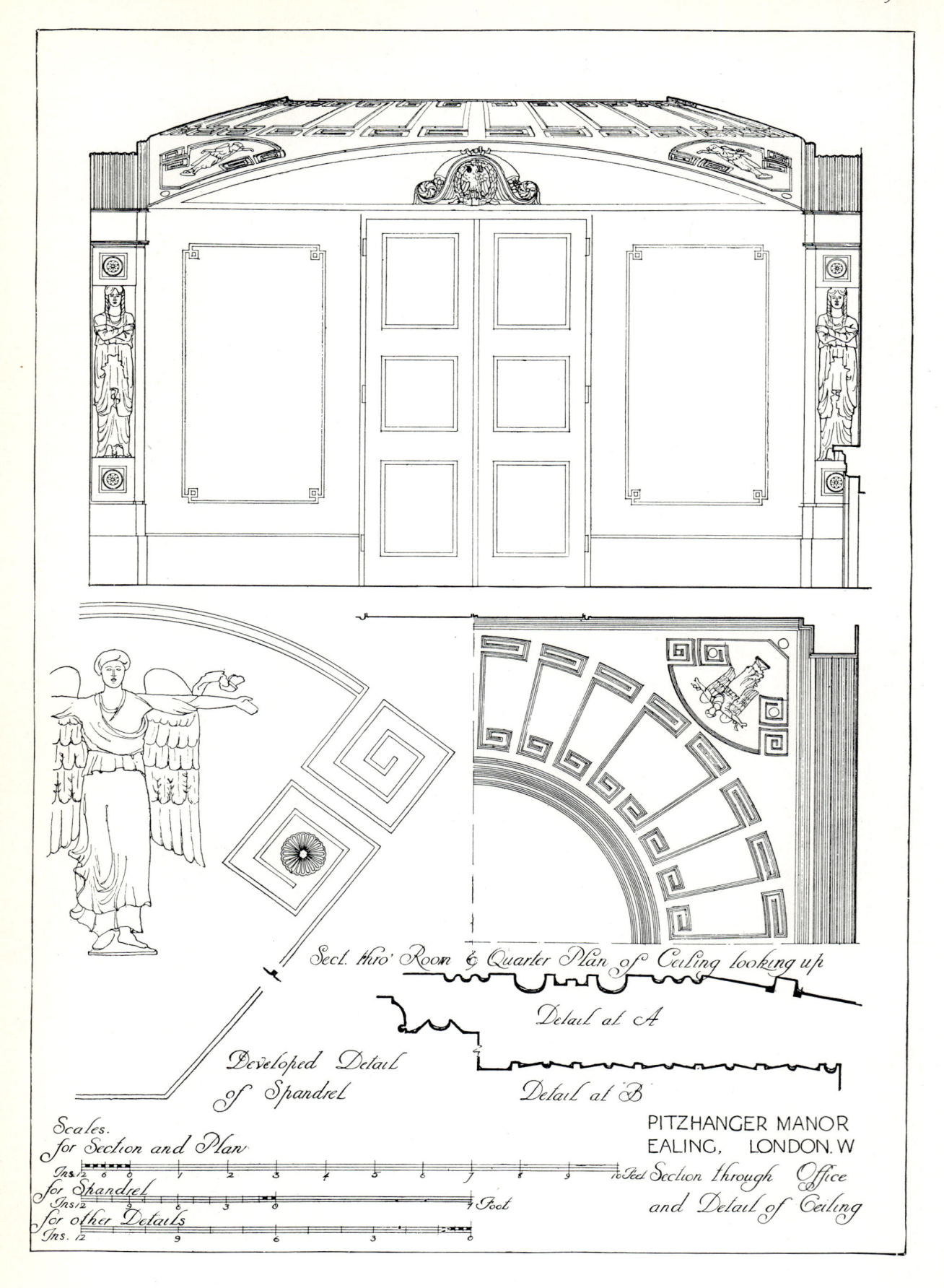

Sect. thro' Room & Quarter Plan of Ceiling looking up

Detail at A

Developed Detail
of Spandrel

Detail at B

Scales.
for Section and Plan

for Spandrel

for other Details

PITZHANGER MANOR
EALING, LONDON. W

Section through Office
and Detail of Ceiling

Plate 96

Plate 97

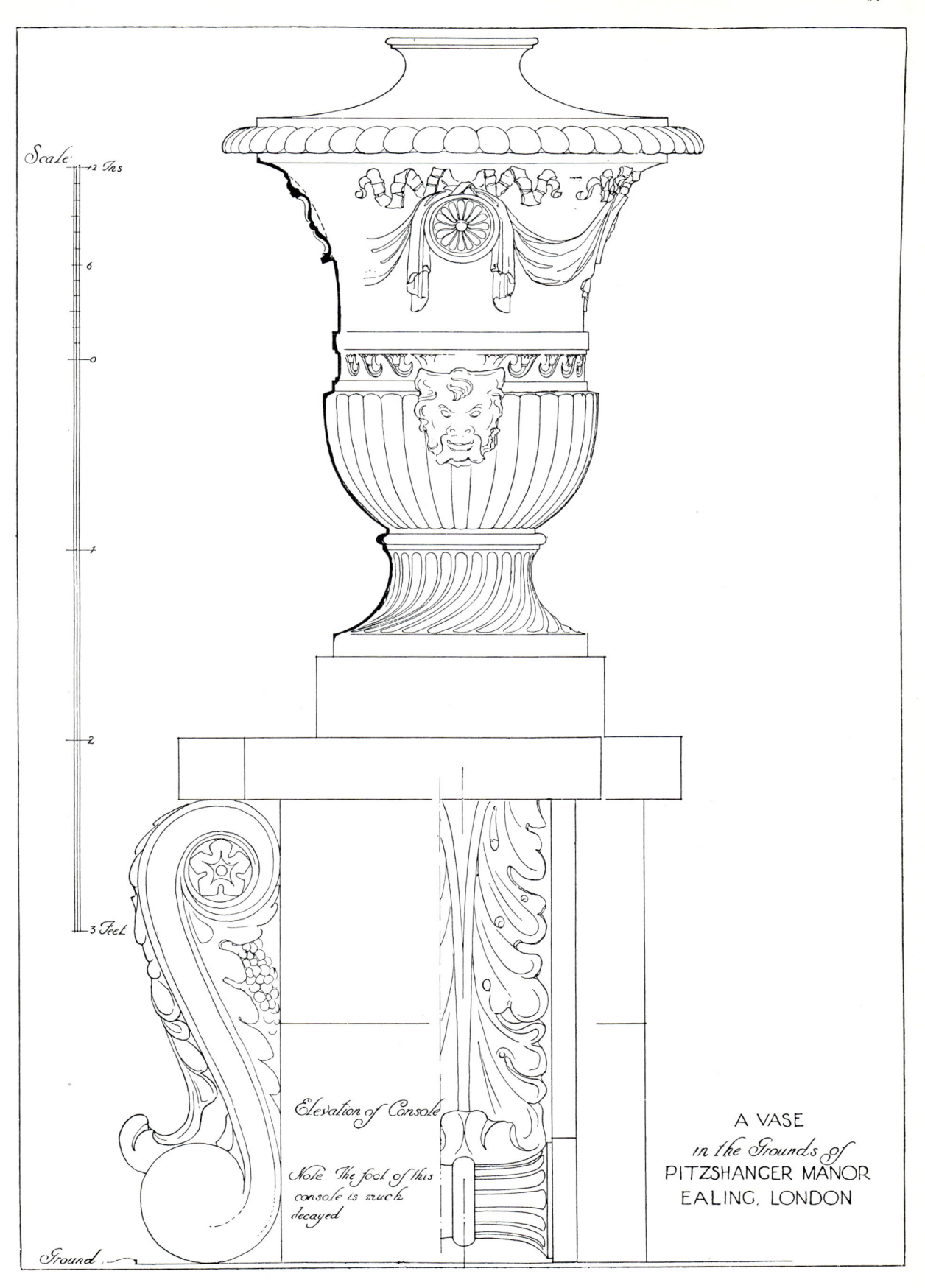

Scale
12 Ins
6
0
1
2
3 Feet
Ground

Elevation of Console

Note the foot of this console is much decayed

A VASE
in the Grounds of
PITZSHANGER MANOR
EALING, LONDON

Plate 98

Section

Elevation

Upper Part of
Door altered
and glazed

Plan

Patera & Flutes in Frieze

Plan through Architrave of Door-opening

Base of Column

Detail of Order.

PORCH from the
MANOR HOUSE
HAM, SURREY.
Elevation & Details

Scale for Details

Scale for Elevation

Plate 99

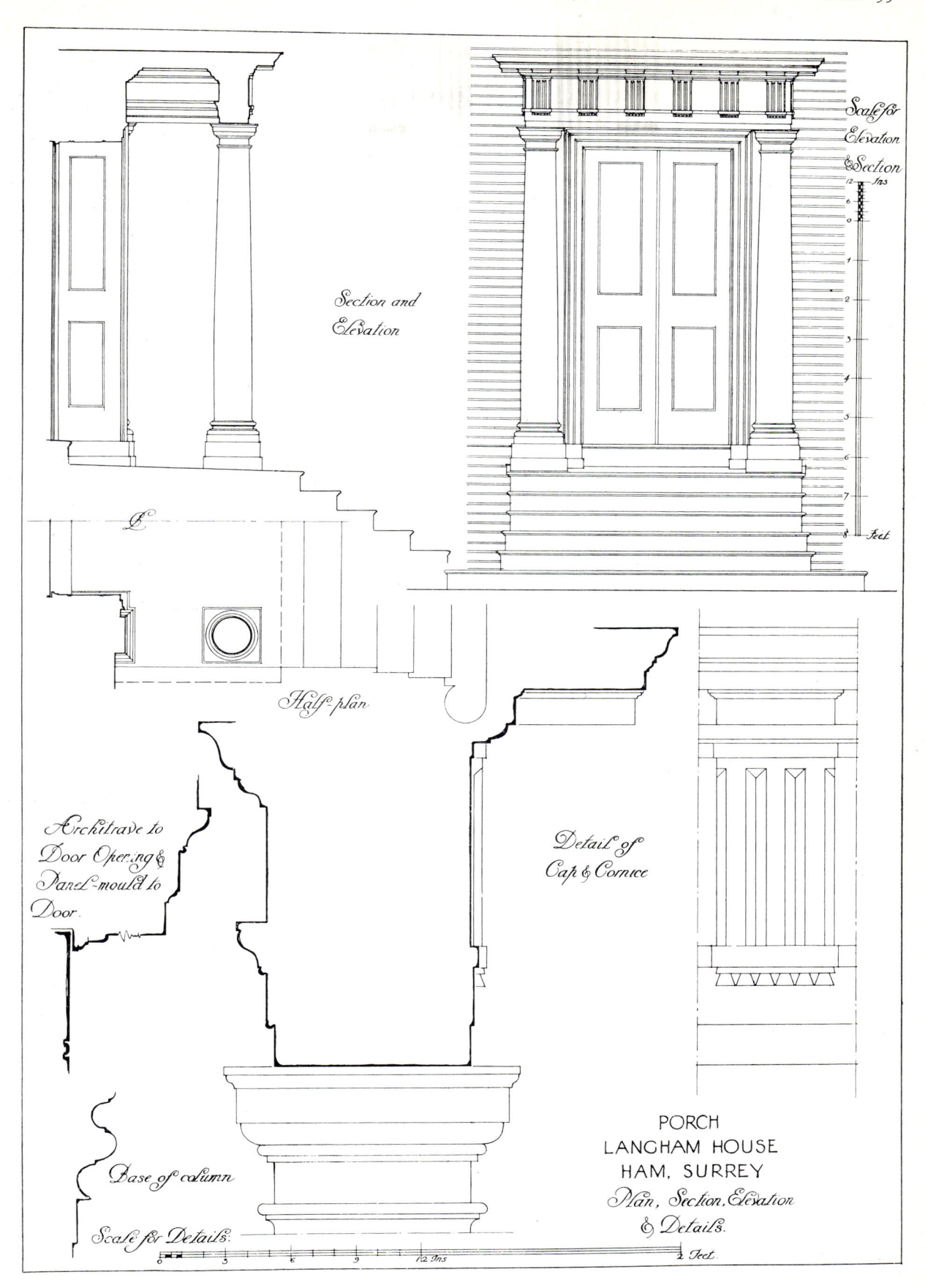

Section and Elevation

Scale for Elevation & Section

Half-plan

Architrave to Door Opening & Panel-mould to Door.

Detail of Cap & Cornice

Base of column

Scale for Details.

PORCH
LANGHAM HOUSE
HAM, SURREY

Plan, Section, Elevation & Details.

Plate 100

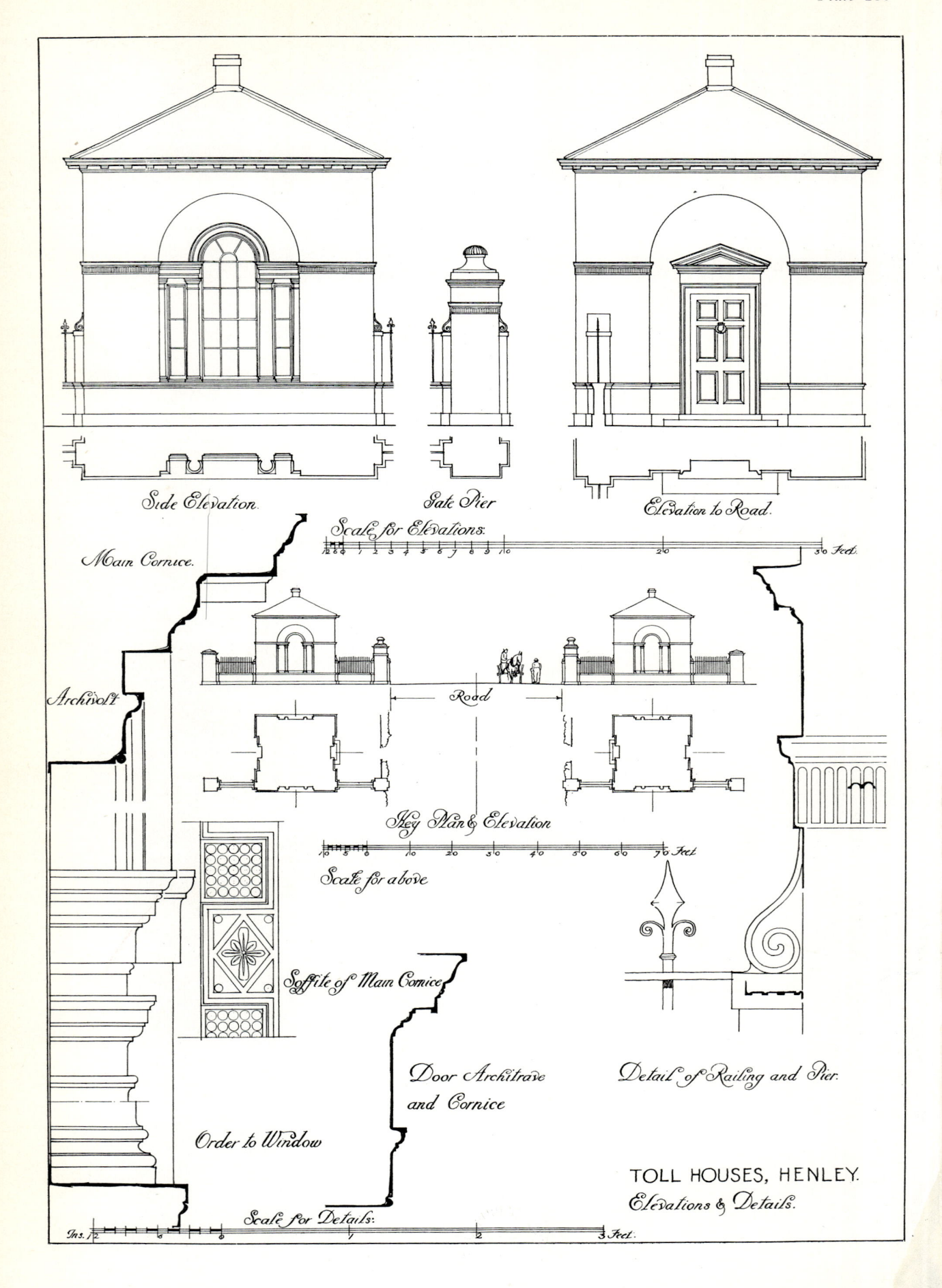

Side Elevation.   Gate Pier.   Elevation to Road.

Scale for Elevations.

Main Cornice.

Archivolt

Road

Key Plan & Elevation

Scale for above

Soffite of Main Cornice

Door Architrave and Cornice

Detail of Railing and Pier.

Order to Window

TOLL HOUSES, HENLEY.
Elevations & Details.

Scale for Details.